W9-AQF-231

CONCILIUM

Religion in the Eighties

CONCILIUM

Concilium 160 (10/1982): Moral Theology

UNEMPLOYMENT AND THE RIGHT TO WORK

Edited by
Jacques Pohier
and
Dietmar Mieth

English Language Editor
Marcus Lefébure

T. & T. CLARK LTD.
Edinburgh

THE SEABURY PRESS
New York

December 1982
T. & T. Clark Ltd., 36 George Street, Edinburgh EH2 2LQ
ISBN: 0 567 30040 4

The Seabury Press, 815 Second Avenue, New York, NY 10017
ISBN: 0 8164 2391 1

Library of Congress Catalog Card No.: 81 85847

Printed in Scotland by William Blackwood & Sons Ltd., Edinburgh

Concilium: Monthly except July and August
Subscriptions 1982: UK and Rest of the World £27·00, postage and handling included; USA and Canada, all applications for subscriptions and enquiries about *Concilium* should be addressed to The Seabury Press, 815 Second Avenue, New York, NY 10017, USA.

CONTENTS

Part I
The Situation in the Western World
A. Factors in the Development of Unemployment

B. The Right to Work

C. Towards a New Theology of Work

Part II
Questions from the Third World to the 'Christian West'

Editorial

Is the Third World separated from the West by an Abyss?

IN 1982, it is not necessary to explain why unemployment and the right to work deserve the attention of moral theology; it is obvious. It is equally obvious that the problems are too great to be dealt with in a journal of this size. We were faced with the need for a choice and we decided to devote the major part of this issue to the way in which the problems of unemployment and the right to work exist in the West (Europe and North America) since it is a fact, whether or not you deplore this, that the vast majority of the readers of *Concilium* are westerners.

However, we decided to devote the last part of this issue to the manner in which these problems arise in the Third World. In making this decision, we did not intend to imply that, out of compassion, we were giving the Third World space in the form of an appendix, which had, however, no follow-up. On the contrary, our attention was to demonstrate, by a vigorous challenge from the Third World, that from a strictly egocentric point of view, the way in which the West views the problems of unemployment and the right to work is unrealistic and ineffective, and that from the point of view of ethics or the Gospel, it is immoral and anti-Christian.

Now, the most difficult point for the West to grasp seems to be that the difference between the Third World and the West, as far as unemployment and the right to work are concerned, is not only one of quantity and degree, but also one of quality and nature. That holds not only for the fact that considerable quantitative differences end up by introducing differences of nature, but also that unemployment and the right to work are part of a completely different economic, social, and human context. In order to understand the Third World, therefore, it is not enough for the West to make some changes in quantity or degree to its way of viewing the problems. It will have to make a qualitative change to the very nature of it. And that is just as true for the West's theology, ethics and pastoral care as for economics and politics.

We leave that for you to judge. We wanted to begin this issue with a description of the present factors of the change in work and unemployment in the West: new technical conditions (*Puel*), new economic data (*Gorz*), and the consequences of unemployment for the psychology of the individual and the group (*Heimler*). What is the dominant impression to emerge from these articles (and also from *Fetscher's* contribution on the transformation which has taken place in the meaning of work)? It is that the West's fundamental problem is to look for the meaning of work outside work or beyond it much more than in work itself. We are obviously not denying the fact that work can have both an individual and collective value in itself, but above all, we are seeking to regulate the effects of work (and unemployment) on the lives of individuals and groups by encouraging life without work and putting working life at the service of life outside it. Puel, Gorz and Heimler have very different concerns, methods and theories and put forward analyses and solutions which are sometimes contradictory (coming from such specialists, these contradictions should encourage modesty in the theologians and pastors who, in the name of the 'necessary social witness of the Christian faith' propose or call for a very systematic and sound theology of work). However, these contradictions do not prevent them from agreeing that, faced with the growth of unemployment, the solution is to be found not in more work for everyone, but in a different distribution of the mass of work available, so as to create a new economy and provide a livelihood for the individual, and in giving work a different role in the life of individuals and groups.

On this point, the situation is radically different in the Third World. There, people do not look outside or beyond work, but for work. They do this side of work, and there, its meeting is quite simple and does not demand long study, i.e., so that oneself and one's children will not starve. Their societies do not manage to increase the amount of work to be divided among the potential workforce, and this existing amount is neither enough to ensure the running of the economy nor enough to provide individuals and groups with a basic livelihood. Thus, the situation is the absolute opposite of that in the West.

As for the subject which we wanted to take for the second part of this issue, the emergence of the right to work, the difference between the situation in the West and that in the Third World is not any less. *Krietemeyer* gives an example of this emergence by stating that the right to work has been incorporated in US Federal legislation since the Thirties and the New Deal. We were lucky and honoured that the well-known official organisation, the International Labour Organisation (ILO) in Geneva is willing to allow us to publish a version (probably not yet the final version) of the report which the ILO is preparing for the International Conference on Work which will take place in 1983. The subject matter of this conference is just this right to work and the possible revision of the Convention and/or recommendation No. 122 of 1964 on the politics of employment. The tripartite conference will bring together the government representatives, employers and working people from the member countries. We should like to extend our heartfelt thanks to the ILO for having allowed us to publish part of this report in advance. Finally, *Hengsbach* studies the way in which the right to work appears in the thought and action of Christians and the ecclesial authorities.

You will perhaps feel that we are attaching too much importance to institutions, i.e., governments, international institutions and the Church, and not enough to the daily and persistent struggles which more than a century of the emergence of the right to work has occasioned. Where in this issue are the strikes, hardships and deaths which were the price of these struggles? Who would guess from this journal that May Day, 1st May, the celebration of which is so widespread in 'socialist' and in certain 'capitalist' countries (and recovered by the Roman Catholic Church in the Feast of St Joseph, patron saint of working people), commemorates the many dead from the savage repression of a strike in the USA? We are well aware of this omission and regret it.

However, for all that, we should not like the institutional aspect to be under-estimated. On the one hand, because if a right is not recognised, assured and guaranteed by a society's institutions in real life, it remains in the realm of the purely abstract. As long as the right to work is not embodied in practice and in the institutions, it remains a pious hope. On the other hand, as Lacordaire so magnificently expressed it, 'between the rich and the poor, the powerful and the weak, it is liberty which oppresses and the law which liberates'. In fact, if there is no legislation which is respected, the rich and the powerful can do what they like, and the poor and the weak have no other possible way of defending themselves against the former other than turning to revolt which is often sterile and impotent. This is what is universally called, 'the free play of the laws of free trade' or 'liberalism'. We need rights, legislation and case-law to re-establish equilibrium. If you doubt this, a look at who resists the establishment of a right to work, and the reasons why and how, will suffice.

Here again, the situation of the Third World is once again the opposite of that of the West. As *Fernandes* and *de Souza* very well illustrate, the basic characteristic of employment in the Third World is the predominance of the unorganised 'informal' sector. The fact that in the Third World work is not only unorganised in rural areas but also in the huge, teeming urban centres makes the emergence of any right to work (including any employment legislation) impossible and unthinkable. There, work is not a right, but almost subject to chance and always to luck. In any case, in most of these countries, no authority would have the means to impose a law of this kind on anyone. Obviously, it is not at all difficult to declare that the right to work is a universal right. However, at this level, it remains wholly in the realm of the abstract and will only be effective when the world of work, on the one hand, and the world of institutions, on the other hand, carry some weight. To speak of a right to work in some countries is just as anachronistic and out of place as to speak of a right to consume in those countries where there is nothing to consume.

For all that, do we have to renounce any attempt to develop a theology of work which could inspire Christian ethics in its approach to the problems of unemployment and work? We do not think so. That is why we asked *I. Fetscher* to take up the anthropological and theological range of changes in the meaning of work in our western society, and *D. Mieth* to emphasise the social and Christian extent of solidarity which, in the field of a right to work and unemployment, should be a basic reality much more than a basic concept. We also asked *G. Piana* to draw out the diversity of meaning given to work by the Christian tradition. The pastors, the theologians and the faithful who demand that a theology of work should be produced quickly, which would be well suited to present circumstances, well-structured, obviously of universal significance, and which would leave no more room for question or doubt, seem to forget that work has enjoyed very different reputations in Christianity down through the centuries, sometimes very bad, sometimes very good. Is work blessed or is it cursed? Is it the imitation of God, the creator, or the curse of God on the sin of Adam?

Yet, however indispensable these reflections may be, they do not exempt Western Christians from being open to questioning by the radical originality of the unemployment problem and the right to work in the Third World. That is why we wanted the last part of this issue to be given over to Third World authors so that they are able to tell their Christian brothers in the West what is what and invite them to open their eyes, for the West is frightened of dying of its unemployment, whereas there is a much greater danger that it will, in turn, die of the unemployment which would kill the Third World. We asked the team at the *Indian Social Institute* in *New Delhi* to present the specific nature of the employment and unemployment problem in the Third World. We received a very long article from Brazil (*Beozzo*), but despite its great interest, we were only able to publish a striking excerpt which allows you to see what it means to be a rural worker in Brazil today. Although it is cut off from its logical end, we are pleased that this extract closes by setting out the struggle which the Brazilian Church is undertaking on behalf of the landless and starving peasants. The logic of the Gospel in this struggle is clarified by the article written by a theologian who knows what he is talking about in view of his life in Nicaragua and El Salvador (*Ellacuria*). Unemployment is a challenge for the kingdom of God. For our part, being westerners, we must finish this editorial by putting forward our strictly personal opinion.

It seems to us that the West views the problems of unemployment and the right to work with an almost suicidal short-sightedness. Whether one takes a stand from a demographic, technical, economic or financial point of view, etc., it is becoming unrealistic and stupid to view the problems of unemployment and the right to work in the West as if they were independent of the manner in which they are viewed in the Third World. Even from a strictly egocentric point of view, this would in itself be a major error of judgment. From an ethical point of view, this is more than an error, it is an offence. And from a Christian point of view, it is more than an offence, it is a sin. We are well aware that such statements, no matter how categorical and sincere, carry virtually no weight in the face of the very complex mechanisms and socio-economic forces which determine the problem of unemployment. We are well aware that they are weak beside the crushing suffering which unemployment means for so many millions of human beings. We also know that they carry ridiculous little weight faced with the selfishness of the world's rich countries, who are too occupied with the ruthless economic war into which they have been thrown, and also faced with the ethnic centrism of all the parties concerned. History teaches us that similar upheavals to those demanded by such a state of affairs are virtually never brought about by humanity and peace, but by struggle, war, violence and blood.

Therefore, we personally believe that the formidable upheaval, with a rational, just and Christian way of viewing the problem of unemployment and the right to work should demand, will not come about without international confrontation and terrible catastrophe. Do we perhaps find ourselves before the fall of Rome, the fall of Byzantium or perhaps the fall of the *ancien régime*? As Christians, we hope (in the theological meaning of this word) that the slightest efforts made in an attempt to facilitate this process and to limit the inevitable wastage will not be totally in vain. This issue of *Concilium* aspires to be no more than a drop in the ocean. However, a drop is a drop, and the ocean is made up of drops. May this issue provoke other people to join with those who are already there, to produce a little trickle of hope.

JACQUES POHIER
DIETMAR MIETH

Translated by Pauline A. Stuart

PART I

The Situation in the Western World
A. Factors in the Development of Unemployment

Hugues Puel

New Technical Conditions of Work and the Problems of Employment

THINKING AS a moralist about the new technical conditions of work and problems of employment requires one to have mastered a field in which research has been particularly abundant, not only in France, but also in all the major industrial nations. Even after working on this question for twenty years, both in research and teaching, I cannot claim an exhaustive knowledge. Despite all effort to investigate the complexity of the data and the analyses, an attempt to give an overall picture remains presumptuous, with the danger of oversimplification ever present.

To come directly to the point and give a short answer to the question, we may say that technology has a twofold effect on work. There is an *effect of constraint*, because methods of work have been radically modified by the intervention of technology, and an *effect of enrichment*, because the productivity of work has been considerably increased. For us the ethical question therefore has a twofold aspect, winning freedom in relation to the technical systems and the demand for a share in the process of enrichment.

1. THE EFFECT OF CONSTRAINT

Technology transforms the relations of man and nature. This modern phenomenon is also ancient history. When the human race was forced by demographic pressure to abandon the mode of production of the hunter-gatherers, it had the feeling of losing by the deal and turning its back on the society of abundance.[1] Three or four hours a day devoted to hunting and fishing which had acquired a very large element of play had satisfied the tribe's needs for agricultural work. While it made possible an improved ratio of productivity between man and space, the neolithic revolution must have been felt as a constraint because *per capita* productivity had not yet risen sufficiently. This required techniques of irrigation which made possible a considerable improvement in yields, but at the cost of technological and political control of the system of irrigation. These amounted to new constraints: the economies of irrigated agriculture are societies of slavery and oriental despotism.[2]

The industrial revolution produced an even greater transformation in the relations of man and nature, and brought with it a quota of new constraints. With it more powerful energy sources were discovered and harnessed. Whether deriving from coal mines, dams, oil deposits or the shattering of uranium, the genie electricity multiplied productive capacities a hundredfold. Many raw materials were exploited and transformed. Mechanisation totally changed production processes. Automation was not far behind. The first and then the second industrial revolutions, followed by the automation of production processes, have changed the whole content of work. Within this movement of industrialisation, three main systems of work succeeded each other, though they still co-exist today:

—the 'man-product' system, in which the worker intervenes directly on matter and in the creation of the product with the help of simple, generally manual, tools;
—the 'man-machine' system, in which the worker uses machines and devices adapted for one or more specific technical operations, while retaining physical contact with the material being worked;
—the 'machine-product' system, in which the production installations initiate processes of transformation in which the installations are activated by the operators from control centres where the essential elements of the transformation process are symbolised but the workers have no physical contact with the product.[3]

This third system of work is spreading rapidly at present with the growth of automation, NC (numeric control) machines, the use of robots and the development of electronics.

However, the logic of the industrial revolution is also spreading to the immense service sector, into which data-processing and all the techniques of communication and electronics are making huge inroads. The white-collar world, the tertiary sector, dominates banking institutions, insurance companies, state bureaucracies, social organisations, public, semi-public and private administrations. The logic of functional organisations which made possible mass production is spreading to a large part of service activities, from transport to telecommunications, from banking to large-scale commerce, from tourism to scientific research. These are the new working conditions for the majority of the working population in the industrialised and urbanised countries.

New conditions, new conditionings: working conditions have been transformed and constraints have multiplied. No document has expressed this movement of the industrial revolution better than the *Communist Manifesto*:

> All that is solid melts into air, all that is holy is profaned, and man is at last compelled to face with his sober senses his real conditions of life and his relations with his kind. . . . Owing to the extensive use of machinery and to division of labour, the work of the proletarians has lost all individual character, and, consequently, all charm for the workman.[4]

Taylorism and the scientific organisation of work have broken down the worker's movements. Systems analysts strip the proletariat of its skill. Administrative work no less than industrial labour is forced into the framework of the organisation. There can be little doubt about this growth of constraints. It is strongly felt by all those who live in an industrial and urban environment and at almost every level. The alternative and ecological movements exploit this feeling when they appeal to the nostalgia for a world seen as more human because freer from constraint, that of the village and rural society. There could be a great deal of discussion here because, while they were different, the constraints of traditional rural society were not for all that less powerful, and urban society, while it imposes new constraints, also offers new freedoms. But the point we need to discuss is different: is this growth of constraints, whether real or partly imaginary, due to the development of technology?

This debate is fundamental in itself, and fundamental also as a preliminary to the moral question. Is the effect of constraint which we are trying to analyse to be ascribed to technology or to something else? A strong current of radical or left-wing thinking regards constraint as a product of the capitalist nature of our societies. André Gorz writes: 'The fragmentation and specialisation of tasks, the division between intellectual and manual labour, the monopolisation of science by élites, the scale of plants and the centralisation of power which flows from this, none of this is necessary to efficient production. It is necessary, on the other hand, to perpetuate the domination of capital.'[5] And yet these techniques are spreading in societies with different economic systems (the European and Asian socialist countries, the countries of the Third World) and seem to produce the same effects of constraint there. Other writers therefore insist on the cultural roots of our industrial societies. According to them, they rest on a technological mentality characterised by efficiency as a criterion of selection and scientific rationality as a basis for decision. At the root there is a desire for power pushing towards the birth and development of techno-structures: a new type of economic, social and political organisation is transforming these societies into mega-machines. Regimentation and constraints are more the product of organisational power than of technology itself, or technology has been intimately refashioned by its promoters' desire for power.[6]

This debate is complex and difficult because it bears on the nature of science and technology. What is the relationship between the logic of skill and knowledge which is at the base of science and the logic of power which necessarily intersects it because it results in technology and intervention in economic and social life?[7] Nevertheless it is an essential debate for moral discernment because it stresses the possibility that models of the division of labour and hierarchical structures related to the same technological system may be socially relative. Analysing constraint and attempting to feel its force is the first step in the search for liberation.

2. THE EFFECT OF ENRICHMENT

The technological revolution is impelled by powers and engenders constraints, but it transforms the relations of man and nature in the struggle against scarcity. This is the underlying movement of both the neolithic revolution and the industrial revolution, in which demographic pressure almost certainly played a great part. The consequent effect of enrichment is clear. It is visible, even spectacular. And, despite the social and human cost of these upheavals, the balance is indisputably positive.

This statement may shock those who think of the toil of men and women at work, but the fact is that technology has conferred on human labour a productivity which is totally unprecedented. Even a few decades ago, one peasant fed three to five people. The agricultural worker of the developed countries feeds forty to sixty today. The great factory devised by Ford made possible the mass production and distribution of new semi-durable consumer goods (cars, refrigerators, washing-machines, radio and television sets, hi-fi systems, videos) to a wider and wider public. Once the privilege of narrow élites, access to education, to culture and to travel never ceases to spread. The development of the means of mass communication and the dissemination of messages by our planet's artificial satellites open further perspectives for knowledge, communication and cultural exchange. The contradictions, the horrors and the waste of our world should not obscure this enormous effect of enrichment due to technology.

'We haven't got anything out of it.' Modern town-dwellers may well take the same disillusioned view when they compare their lot with that of the villagers of the past as the neolithic farmer dreaming of his ancestors who could live by hunting and gathering. The past is always golden, and paradise always behind us. The other myth, that of indefinite progress and communism on earth, is simply the futuristic version of the first, and little better. It diverts us from moral discernment, which must be based on a judgment about the reality of today.

But what is the reality of this enrichment? A reality attested by the measuring instruments of our statistics of production, agricultural production, industrial production, production of services. All the indicators show the rapidity of growth. During the period 1950-1970 production tripled in many developed countries, and since then a number of Third World countries have plunged into the race for growth.[8] What we call the economic crisis reflects, not a decline in production, but a reduction in growth rates, which is, after all, something very different from what happened in the Thirties and in the cyclical crises of the nineteenth century. Our productive systems have acquired power and adaptability thanks to the whole organisational context on which their functioning depends: modern management techniques with analytical accounting, marketing techniques, methods of financing and State support.

To say that the enrichment is real does not mean that all the apparent enrichment is real. In every statistic there is an effect of illusion resulting from the bias of the measure. In relation to enrichment the illusion may come from the extension of the realm of commodities. Every new exchange value may be counted as pure enrichment when it may simply be the incorporation into the exchange circuit of a pre-existing use-value: an example is the monetarisation in modern society of a number of services which used to be given freely, on the basis of free exchange within the community, in the system of traditional society. Nevertheless, even when this illusion has been removed the increase in the productivity of labour leaves a net positive balance.

Neither does it mean when we say that the enrichment is real that it operates without malfunction or unjust distribution. Technical progress creates wealth, but it is also said to create unemployment. The history of the working-class movement is studded with revolts against machines. Mechanisation eliminates the worker. What enriches some—the owners of the machines—impoverishes others—the workers thrown out of work. But revolts by workers against machines tend to be a feature of the beginning of the industrial revolution. The trade union movement gradually incorporated the advances in productivity resulting from the new technical conditions into its strategy by obtaining wage increases. The calculation was realistic to the extent that it is a matter of observation that technical progress creates many more jobs than it destroys. Since the industrial revolution began to affect Great Britain, Germany, France, the USA, Japan and many other countries, the number of jobs has never stopped rising. The growth of unemployment, when it occurs, is due to other factors, population increase and the extension of the demand for jobs to other sectors of the population. These include those who abandon their traditional independent activities in agriculture or the artisanate to take up waged employment in industry and services, women who add waged employment to their unremunerated domestic work, and all the internal and external immigrants who try to improve their lot by means of a less meagre and less precarious source of income.

The idea that technological progress creates unemployment persists because that is certainly the apparent effect. All over the place workers are experiencing reorganisation of production, factory closures and modernisation which throw some of their number out of work. But the reasons for these changes are not simply technical, but also economic, with the strategies of large firms in search of profit playing an essential role. Moreover, they do result in advances in productivity which have positive effects up and down the chain of production. Up the chain because the new machines and the new processes must themselves be produced and provide work for other branches of industry, both those engaged in producing capital goods and research and development and applied research. Down the chain this is even truer because increased productivity is translated into additional profit which potentially results in new investment which creates new jobs. It is also distributed in the form of an increase in total earnings, and this increased purchasing power reinforces a demand for goods and services which has a positive effect on employment—and a strongly positive one in the case of services which are labour-intensive. If the apparent effect of technical progress in destroying jobs corresponded with reality, it would be impossible to understand how the net job balance could be heavily positive in the long term. The explanation is the effects up and down the production chain of advances in productivity, effects which can be revealed only by analysis.

The point of this argument is not to deny the malfunction which unemployment represents. Another article in this issue will demonstrate its human and social cost.[9] This malfunction can, however, be reduced by appropriate social and economic policies. The institutional suppression of the problem as practised in the USSR and the Central European socialist economies can hardly be regarded as ideal, it is true. It has no evident advantage in terms of working conditions because it has an economic cost resulting from the very considerable loss of productivity to which it gives rise. This phenomenon can be measured by the differences in living standards, which the peoples of these countries feel to their cost. The facts of unemployment must be freely available. Technological progress plays a crucial role in it because it has both positive and disruptive effects on employment. It leads to transformations of the productive system the human cost of which depends on economic and institutional factors. The moral question here is framed in terms of control and sharing.

Advances in productivity mean a surplus to share. The question of distribution is at the heart of our problem. Who gets the wealth produced?

The question is discussed in all the public debates of the democratic countries. Contradictory principles are put forward which often result in particular compromises which are often challenged, as shown by the shifts of power in the major democratic countries. Should unemployment benefits be raised at the risk of discouraging people from looking for work? In some developed countries social expenditure redistributes nearly 30 per cent of the national income; can it rise further without putting businesses in difficulty and discouraging their activities? Should income tax be made more progressive, or does this risk curbing the initiative of the more dynamic? Social needs are immense: how far can we go in redistribution and the reduction of inequalities? Economic policies are based on the answers to these questions. Can the economy be revived by stimulating demand which makes it possible to satisfy certain social needs but may also jeopardise the ability of businesses to invest, and the balance of payments? Alternatively is the answer to be found in supply-side policies, reducing the proportion of wages in the national income in order to allow business to make profits which can then be invested to create new jobs? The risk here is a fall in demand which will depress the consumer goods industries and discourage investment. All these questions arise out of the present economic crisis. They call for solutions through economic policies in which the role of technology is an essential element and in which moral questions are necessarily present.

3. THE MORAL QUESTIONS

Given the effect of constraint and the effect of enrichment, the moral questions raised are those of the conquest of freedom and the demand for sharing.

A society without constraints is not a Utopia to be longed for. Human freedom comes into being in the acceptance of constraints, though these cannot be too heavy, as they still are for too many people. Any demystification of science, technology and economics is valuable here. The development and spread of knowledge in these areas is potentially liberating. The spread of education can make a contribution to this. All movements critical of science and all opposition to forms of energy or processes which seem harmful to workers can be significant as stimuli to reflection. The vigorous debates about big rural or urban developments, industrial or tertiary projects can help to increase awareness. A similar function is filled within workplaces by health and safety committees and the introduction of new ways of organising work: semi-autonomous production units, production rhythms better adapted to the physiological needs of the human body, a reduction in working hours and greater flexibility in hours, work-sharing schemes. It is true that the imperative of productivity remains primary, at least in the modern sector of the economy, but productivity itself makes possible experiments with forms of work which lessen the constraints of industrial work and service activities. And alongside the area marked by the law of productivity a whole field of alternative or social economy may develop with production and service units on a more human scale, more convivial in character, forming a more localised economic network and/or to some extent sheltered from the effects of the international division of labour.[10] Here the constraints of productivism will be less powerful, and work will be able to take on greater significance for the individuals who engage in it; those who are excluded from the modern system will be able to find a livelihood. This is an alternative path, in my view a significant one, an effort to put constraints at arm's length. Nevertheless we must be clear that it has an economic cost in that it limits enrichment. There is less to share, but these experiments have the merit of posing forcefully the question what enrichment means.

An economy without scarcity is also not a Utopia to be longed for. It leads to excess which exhausts the resources of the planet, exacerbates conflicts and gives priority to economics over politics and culture. Technological progress, that Promethean weapon in the battle against scarcity, must here find its measure. But morality cannot content itself with preaching an asceticism of desires and needs, whether it is the religious asceticism of the Rule of St Augustine ('It is better to have few needs than many goods') or the secular asceticism of Rousseau ('Every new need forges new fetters'). It is of course open to any individual or any voluntary group to practise such an asceticism. In my opinion, however, the task of morals is to subject enrichment as such to scrutiny on the basis of a fundamental acceptance in an optimistic attitude towards the collective achievement of the human race. This enrichment effect is desirable and good. The means of achieving it may indeed be open to criticism and reform, but enrichment is necessary to meet the explosion of social needs. In particular, the way it is shared requires to be worked out differently. Here the moral question cuts across the political debate, since the forms of sharing are determined not only by increasing control of production and distribution, but also by the intervention of processes of redistribution which affect the delicate balance between the State and civil society.

Moralists can do no more than locate the questions asked by people at work and confronted by the environment of their activity, which is not merely technical but also economic. They must try to listen to the questions in the diversity of situations experienced, conditionings undergone and aspirations aroused. The value of their efforts will depend on their openness to the universal.

Translated by Francis McDonagh

Notes

1. See the book by the American ethnologist Marshall Sahlins *Stone Age Economics.*
2. See the classic work of Karl Wittfogel, *Oriental Despotism* (New Haven 1964).
3. A review in French of all the work on this question was produced in December 1980 by Alain d'Iribarne under the title *Technologie et systèmes du travail: L'évolution du travail face au développement des technologies* for the Journées nationales d'études du Centre d'Etudes et de recherche sur les qualifications (extensive bibliography).
4. Frederick Engels and Karl Marx *The Communist Manifesto* (Penguin ed., London 1967) pp. 83, 87.
5. André Gorz *Critique de la division du travail* (Paris 1973). In support of his argument Gorz includes a partial translation of the famous essay by the radical American economist Stephen Marglin, *What do bosses do?*
6. A selection from a wealth of writing: Jacques Ellul *The Technological Society* (New York 1964); Lewis Mumford *Technics* (London 1967); Alain Birou and Paul Marc Henry *Towards a Redefinition of Development* (Paris 1977).
7. Two issues of *Economie et Humanisme* have dealt with this problem: No. 212 (July-August 1973), 'La science comme pouvoir', and No. 262 (November-December 1981), 'Science et Technologie: des produits sociaux'.
8. See Pierre Judet *Les Nouveaux pays industriels* Paris 1981.
9. See my book *En finir avec le chômage* Paris 1981. And see the article below by Eugene Heimler 'The Emotional Significance of Work'.
10. See the special issue of *Economie et Humanisme* on the social economy, No. 264 (March-April 1982).

André Gorz

New Economic Data of Employment and Unemployment

IN ALL highly industrialised countries, paid work is rapidly ceasing to be the main content of life today. In Western Germany, for example, the number of people who have said that they prefer free time to paid work has increased between 1962 and 1976 from 36 per cent to 56 per cent. In Sweden, the number of those for whom paid work is the most important element in their life has fallen from 33 per cent to 17 per cent, free time increasing from 13 per cent to 27 per cent and the family decreasing from 46 per cent to 44 per cent.

This loss of interest is even more marked among agricultural workers, skilled craftsmen or self-employed people. There are two important reasons for this. They are firstly the disappearance of the skilled crafts or trades and secondly the disappearance of work itself.

1. THE ABOLITION OF THE 'SKILLED CRAFTS'

Traditionally, what is meant by 'skilled craft' has been a complete skill or ability enabling the person possessing it to regard himself as the author of a complete action or job. This skill belonged to the person who possessed it and was perfected by him together with the tools of his trade throughout his active professional life. It was the source of his social identity and his personal development. It was above all cultural. What was useful, beautiful, functional and gratuitous were all closely and indeed intimately intermingled in it.

The skilled crafts began to disappear with the emergence of mass manufacture. The processes initiated by Henry Ford at the beginning of this century led to a speeding up and the crafts have now almost ceased to exist with the coming of automation. Only a very thin layer of highly qualified workers, skilled craftsmen, artists and members of the free professions can still claim to possess a complete craft or trade and can still reply, in answer to the question: 'What do you do for a living?', '*I am* a coach builder' or '*I am* a mason' or '*I am* a paediatrician'.

For the vast majority—at least three-quarters—of paid employees, work is no longer either a skilled, complete craft or a creative occupation that enables the one who carries it out to say: 'I am . . .' or 'I make . . .'. The factory worker who operates the press which stamps out one part of the same car model, the front wings, for example, for months on end cannot say: 'I make wings'. He can only say 'I work the press'. In the same way, the man operating a machine for sticking laminated boards together in a factory producing industrial furniture cannot say: 'I make furniture' or 'I am a carpenter and joiner'. He can only say: 'I work at . . .'.

It is even more difficult for administrators, bank officials, post office employees, those in the so-called service industries and others to identify themselves with their work as something productive. Their work is more often a kind of alienation rather than a giving of themselves. Neither its nature nor its content is determined by the person who does it. Both are determined rather by the social and international division of labour. One of the consequences of this division of labour that takes place nowadays on an increasingly enormous economic scale is that the individual on the one hand no longer produces any of the things that he consumes and that he can, on the other, no longer consume anything that he in fact produces—in so far as the term 'production' still has any meaning for workers in industries with continuous flow and in the calculator and computer industry, for example. Even if they have high qualifications as the result of a long period of training, they cannot use them outside their place of work. They possess a highly specialised and fragmentary skill. They do not in any sense possess a culture, through and within which they can grow and develop throughout their life.

This skill or ability is, moreover, determined by the machines or the apparatus used. It changes as techniques develop, but this change and the retraining that it necessitates does not in any way lead to cultural enrichment, personal progress or even to a professional career for workers on the shop floor.

Like the nature of the products of work, the nature and content of work itself are determined in centres of scientific research in the South of France, Arizona and California. What Marx called the 'socialisation of the process of production' is achieved on a world-wide scale and is a form of internationalisation. In one place there is a factory manufacturing speedometers for the entire car industry of Europe and in another place a whole town is given over to the production of car tyres which are sold throughout the world. Half of Europe's ball-bearings come from two factories situated in medium-sized towns!

No one knows any longer for whom he is working. There may be a certain solidarity among workers in their place of work, but class solidarity among workers in different undertakings within the same town or district is becoming more and more difficult to achieve and is now the exception rather than the rule. This is partly because most undertakings are no longer an integral part of the network of relationships between those who live in the place where the undertaking is situated. Modern enterprises produce goods not for the local inhabitants, but for the world market and often for a large group which is multinational and of which they are sub-contractors or subsidiaries. Many towns have become dormitories, with all their inhabitants working elsewhere. Others resemble colonies, with those who live in them working for absent masters and their governments accepting economic decisions over which they have hardly any control or influence.

If there is to be some degree at least of democratisation, a decentralisation of decision-making and an effective self-administration, each city, region and nation has to be able to produce at least a large part of what it consumes and has to do so in such a way that the population can be given at least some share in the decisions made with regard to production, consumption and the organisation of labour.

Any attempt to restore a degree of autonomy at the local level is, however, confronted with certain serious limitations which can hardly be overcome and which are in fact inherent in the 'socialisation of the process of production' to which I have referred above and which is always implied in any form of industrial production. Even as commonplace an apparatus as a washing-machine, for example, involves in its design and manufacture a complex of techniques that far exceeds the abilities of a group or even a whole community of several thousand people! Each of the parts of which it consists—the drum, the steel frame, the enamelled plates, the electric motor, the rubber belt, the programmer and so on—are all products of very different technologies and industries. Each of these industries, moreover, uses different machines—for laminating, wire-drawing, stamping, enamelling, winding, making pipes, etc.—and many other industries have to exist in order to design and produce them.

Going back still further in this process, many other factors are involved, including the transmission, classification and teaching of all these skills, the extraction of raw materials and the transport of half-finished products. All these call for a further complex of establishments and services and therefore for a very diversified form of society with a great deal of division of labour and specialisation.

It therefore only seems to be possible to achieve self-administration, the practice of complete skilled crafts and relationships based on mutual agreement, solidarity and voluntary co-operation, outside the framework of large-scale socialised production. Automation and information storage and retrieval may help to eliminate repetitive and monotonous tasks, but they will not get rid of the heteronomous nature of paid work that is determined by so many different factors.

Automation and data processing may also make it easier for light industries to be more widely distributed so that there can be more small factories producing complete articles locally and taking into account the local needs and preferences. There must, however, be a strong political desire for the deconcentration of industry before it can even begin to take place. It would in fact destroy the uniform nature of the market and of fashion and would undermine the power that the great firms have today to impose their products on a mass of consumers who have been exposed to their influence for so long and made uniform in their tastes. It would also remove its technical obstacles that now prevent the development, alongside and in place of paid work and large-scale production of trade, of small-scale activities and means of production based on co-operation and free association and even domestically based industries with their new work culture and their new spirit of mutual self-help and co-operation. This development may be technically possible, but it can never begin as the result of a merely spontaneous growth, because it is dependent in the first place on both the great firms and central governments relinquishing some of the political, economic and ideological power that they have held for so long.

2. TOWARDS THE ABOLITION OF WORK?

The great technological changes that are still taking place are also making employment itself and the qualifications that it calls for very insecure. Most employed persons under the age of fifty must expect nowadays to have to gain new qualifications and even change to other kinds of work several times in the course of their working life. It is almost impossible for most people today to be deeply attached to or to identify themselves with the employment or the job that they 'have' and this is an additional reason why they look outside their paid work, in leisure-time activities, family life or various forms of social or political activity, to fulfil their need for personal achievement.

This shifting of the centre of gravity in personal life from paid work to unpaid and non-trading activities will be greatly accelerated by automation however little the cultural and institutional obstacles to it are removed. Automation and data storage and retrieval are at present drawing our attention to a distinction between three rights that we have so far tended to regard as a single right. These are firstly the *right to work*, secondly the *right to paid employment* and thirdly the *right to an income*.

The disjunction between the right to a job and the right to an income has virtually been achieved at least in Western Europe by the indirect means of granting unemployment benefit and arranging for early retirement. In Northern Europe, it is becoming increasingly common to pay the unemployed 70 per cent of the previous salary or wages without imposing any length of time on this payment. In France, workers employed in areas experiencing economic hardship can be retired at the age of fifty-five or even fifty and still receive 80 per cent of their salary or wages.

The fundamental problem is not, however, solved simply by dealing with the right of those who are unemployed to an income. The granting of unemployment benefit to the unemployed in fact means that they have an obligation to remain permanently unemployed and that is something that cannot be justified, as it clearly does violence to those on whom it is imposed.

The economic argument that is generally used to justify it is that it is necessary to maintain the employment—by which is implied the full-time employment in accordance with the legal norms that are in force at the time—of those who continue to produce goods for the market. What is in fact maintained, however, is above all the nature of the social relationships of production between employers and employees. These relationships can only continue in their present form so long as employment remains the chief activity of paid workers. The power that employers have over the work of those whom they employ and pay is felt by the latter as a power over their lives and as a form of existential dependence and subservience. If, on the other hand, my paid work—thirty hours a week or less—leaves me the time and if society gives me the means to perform activities outside my employment which are as important to me as—or even more important than—that paid employment, then my existential and hierarchical relationships with my employer will be profoundly changed. He will no longer be dealing with a labour force that simply accepts his power and his decisions without question.

The resistance of industrial society to any general attempt to reduce the length of their working life derives mainly, but not, of course, exclusively from this. Distribution of the reduced time in the most unequal way, by creating full employment for some workers and complete unemployment for others, which is the most unequal distribution, reinforces a greater sense of insecurity felt by the paid worker and the relationship of domination.

The number of hours spent at work in order to ensure a given level of production is in any case rapidly being reduced by automation and the use of data processing—so quickly, in fact, that the question of man's right to work as distinct from his right to paid employment is already threatening to become acute. According to a study undertaken by the Stanford Research Institute and presented in March 1979 to the Congress of American Automobile Workers (UAW), 80 per cent of manual work, that is twenty million manual jobs out of a present total of twenty-five million, in the industry will have been automated before the end of this century. There has, to my knowledge, not yet been any similar long-term study of office jobs, but, according to all the forecasts made for the end of 1990, the perspectives do not seem to be very different.

3. TOWARDS A SOCIETY OF FREED TIME?

There are, it would seem, four possible responses at the political and economic level that can be borne in mind with regard to this tendency for work to disappear. We will consider these in order.

In the first place, there is what might be called '*enrolment*'—increasing unemployment can be partly disguised by a generally longer period of full-time education, by compulsory military service and by such methods as the creation of para-military forms of 'work' service, increasing arms production and the provision of jobs on a large scale that are without any obvious social value. Far from restoring the lost right to work to its former status and giving work a new value, all these measures suggest a degree of coercion and give the idea of work penitential and repressive overtones and imply that the State is exerting domination over the population.

Secondly, there is '*tertiarisation*'. The number of service jobs can be increased by transferring activities that people usually do for and by themselves to paid professional workers. These tasks include, for example, health care, care of personal appearance, sexual activity, the bringing up of children, counselling for marriage and family difficulties, professional problems and personal relationships, visiting the sick, comforting the dying and counselling the bereaved. Millions of 'specialised' jobs can thus be created in such a way that each person will provide one normalised service and be a consumer of all the other normalised services, which will in turn be provided by others. This procedure, of course, gives great emphasis to the univalence, the dependence and the heteronomy of each individual and it is in a sense a caricature of certain tendencies that already exist in American society in particular. If it were applied as a serious response to the problem of the disappearance of work, it would reduce still further relationships of mutual giving and increase trade relationships.

We now turn to the third possible response, which is the type of society that tends to come about spontaneously in a situation in which work is rapidly ceasing to exist. This society could be called the '*stratified dual society*' and in it there is, on the one hand, a great number of people who are completely unemployed and, on the other, an aristocracy of protected workers who are an integral part of their firms and who perpetuate an ethos of output, the career ideal and the spirit of competition. Between these two extremes, there is a mass of occasional workers, badly paid, floating, insecure, without status or rights and doing thankless jobs that are always changing and are too difficult to automate or even to mechanise.

Just as American society provides the model of my third response (tertiarisation), Japanese society represents the most advanced stage in this division of economic activity into two distinct spheres—hence the term 'dual economy'. French technocrats have suggested an adaptation of this Japanese model as a solution of the present problem and have given it the name of 'dual socio-economy'. They have argued that the western economies should be divided into a modern sector, which should be exposed to international competition, and a 'protected' sector, within which the mass of the active population should work with a small output and a similarly small payment. mainly in the service industries that do not exert an influence on the prime costs of modern industry.

This 'stratified dual society' consisting of two distinct layers in the population, one subordinate to the other, contains in a concentrated form most of the disadvantages of the first two models ('enrolment' and 'tertiarisation') and, by wasting unproductive work in an organised way, does not deal at all satisfactorily with the central problem raised by automation. That problem is: How can people benefit from the increase in free time that they have as a result of recent technological changes and how can their right to work be safeguarded at the same time?

We come now to the fourth option, that of a '*society of freed time*'. The inherent aim of all industrial societies is to promote the quantitative growth of the wealth that can be produced in one day's work. Every member of such a society can therefore only be assured of full-time employment if he continues to contribute to the undefined growth of that wealth. This undefined growth, however, is neither physically possible nor socially desirable, because it calls for an undefined growth of consumption, with all that is implied in that consumer growth in terms of waste and the cult of goods. Beyond a certain level, it is no longer true to say that higher consumption means a higher standard of living.

When this level is reached or when we go beyond it, as happens in most highly industrialised countries, it becomes almost impossible to maintain full-time paid employment for the whole population and, what is more, it is no longer really necessary to do so. It soon becomes possible for each person to work for only a few hours each day, for two or three days each week, for a few months each year or for between ten and twenty years in the course of a lifetime in order to maintain a standard of living that is accepted by everyone as sufficient. It is interesting to note that four-fifths of the population of the Scandinavian countries regard their standard of living as already sufficiently high and that the Norwegians think that theirs is too high. It is significantly from these countries that the most advanced thinking is coming on the subject of policies for the present period and formulae for a guaranteed income for life.

Man's right to work assumes a completely different complexion when this indispensable work takes up no more than a small part of each individual's time. It no longer means the 'right to be employed for wages or a salary', but rather the right to be active and useful to the community outside the framework of paid work, although there is no vital need for anyone to be so. Instead of meaning the right to *receive* a salary or wages in return for a job, the right to work means the right to *give* part of the time that the community no longer demands from the individual to that community. All those who already have a great deal of time—retired people, those who are partly or fully unemployed, those who, like the New York dockers, work for less than thirty hours a week for wages that are guaranteed for life and others—are now experiencing the reality of the need to give, to give oneself and to be accepted in what one gives as more basic than the need to receive.

Societies whose way of life has been based on trading relationships have been able to narrow down, but not to reduce the sphere of relationships governed by disinterested giving, that is, relationships based on love, friendship, tenderness, affection and solidarity. In such relationships, there is no direct interest involved. If I have an interest in loving you, we may say, I do not love you. Interest is absent from such relationships as it is absent from artistic creation. A 'society of freed time', in which its members' time has been set free from the restraints of paid employment, can develop these activities and forms of work that are completely disinterested and without any essentially utilitarian aim or connection with trade.

This type of society is very different from the kind that I described under the third option, the 'stratified dual society', in which each individual works exclusively in one or other of the two sectors. In a 'society of freed time', each person belongs to both spheres and is always moving from one to the other. He may be active for a while in the sphere of socially determined and necessary work and then move into the sphere of activity which he himself determines and which is not governed by economic necessity.

I have described this second sphere in some detail in my book *Farewell to the Proletariat*, in which I gave it the name of 'sphere of autonomy' and said that its activities could include work connected with the extended family, informal neighbourhood associations, mutual help groups and personal creativity. Within it, there would be voluntary production of goods and services without any commercial aim which could not be the object of social programming and would be properly carried out when individuals and basic communities make decisions about it in accordance with their own wishes and allowing free scope for their imagination. This means, of course, that the instruments used should be permanently available to everyone and that they should be what Ivan Illich called 'convivial'. This will only come about if the whole of society aims consciously to make the 'sphere of autonomy' expand.

Translated by David Smith

Eugene Heimler

The Emotional Significance of Work

1. PAST

MY WORK with the unemployed goes back almost thirty years. In 1955 I reported:[1]

> 'the Welfare State provides many forms of assistance besides financial help for those who are in need of it. All these are most important but should not be considered the final answer to our social problems. The situation is somewhat similar to that of a home where the material needs are provided for the child but where, for various reasons, his emotional needs are not fully met. We have learned a great deal about mental illness and emotional disturbance in the last thirty years, and the Welfare State should now see that besides the many existing services it should also make provision for the emotional needs of the people, who find it necessary to apply for National Assistance (social security).'

Although at that time (1955) there was full employment, it became evident that with the changes that are occurring in our society a completely new attitude and philosophy regarding unemployment may become necessary. For the moment I would like to state that I found it possible to assist many chronically unemployed people into work, even those where originally the motivation was missing. Table I opposite shows the number of people referred by what would be known today as a Social Security Department. Between January 1954 and December 1954 the measurement of 'success' and failure was not based on personal opinion but on the ending of National Assistance (social security). It will also be noted that National Assistance in many cases had been chronic. The Table also gave some idea about the financial savings (1954 values) and it has been estimated that £1,600 saved in forty-one referred cases in one Board area would be in the region of 400 times as great had the experiment been carried out on a national scale in Great Britain, i.e., if each Board office referred forty cases. This in a period of one year would have represented (in 1954 values) a total saving of £600,000. Present figures on this basis would be astronomical.

Reference to financial savings is only relevant to show later how much funds may be available, when considering the financing of possible alternatives to unemployment.

In 1957 I reported [2] that the overall number of referrals to the Health Department where I worked as a PSW (Psychiatric Social Worker) from 1 December 1953 to 1

Table I

Case No.	Date of referral	National assistance ceased	National assistance commenced	Case work or approx. No. of interviews	Remarks	Financial savings up to 20.8.55 £ s d
JANUARY-MARCH						
1	12. 2.54	20. 5.55	6. 9.49	Continuing	—	32 10 0
2	12. 2.54	23. 5.55	12. 7.50	Continuing	—	30 0 0
3	12. 2.54	Current	13. 8.51	Continuing	—	—
4	20. 2.54	5.10.54	Prior to Oct. 1950	2	—	105 0 0
5	22. 2.54	Current	21. 9.50	3	—	—
6	25. 2.54	4. 6.55	9. 2.49	4	—	25 0 0
7	10. 3.54	—	—	—	Transferred to another area	—
8	16. 3.54	Current	Prior to 1949	Continuing	—	—
9	19. 3.54	25. 1.55	19. 8.52	20	—	75 0 0
10	25. 3.54	5.10.54	Jan. 1951	4	—	105 0 0
11	29. 3.54	11.11.54	3.12.51	3	—	93 0 0
APRIL-JUNE						
12	2. 4.54	20. 4.54	5. 2.54	1	—	170 0 0
13	5. 4.54	9. 4.54	Prior to Mar. 1948	1	—	175 0 0
14	1. 4.54	—	—	—	Transferred to another area	—
15	21. 4.54	11. 6.54	5.11.52	8	Admitted to hospital	—
16	May 1954	7. 3.55	5. 3.54	1	—	55 0 0
17	5. 5.54	Current	9. 2. 49	Continuing	—	—
18	12. 5.54	10. 6.54	May 1949	Continuing	—	150 0 0
19	21. 5.54	25. 6.54	Jan. 1953	2	Admitted to hospital	—
20	21. 5.54	Current	20. 8.51	5	—	—
21	3. 6.54	31. 5.55	Nov. 1948	15	*Deceased*	—
22	14. 6.54	25. 5.55	Sept. 1951	Continuing	—	30 0 0
23	18. 6.54	Current	6.11.53	4	—	—
JULY-SEPTEMBER						
24	15. 7.54	28. 1.55	26. 6.53	15	—	67 0 0
25	20. 7.54	Current	20. 1.54	2	—	—
26	26. 7.54	—	—	—	Transferred to another area	—
27	9. 8.54	—	—	—	Transferred to another area	—
28	18. 8.54	Current	3. 3.52	6	—	—
29	24. 8.54	15.10.54	20. 2.53	Continuing	—	93 10 0
30	26. 8.54	15. 4.55	Prior to 1948	8	—	42 10 0
31	26. 8.54	—	—	—	Transferred to another area	—
32	10. 9.54	19. 9.54	Prior to 1950	2	—	120 0 0
33	14. 9.54	Current	14. 9.51	Continuing	—	—
34	15. 9.54	11. 5.55	16. 4.47	—	*Deceased*	—
35	16. 9.54	21.12.55	29. 1.54	3	—	80 0 0
36	30. 9.54	—	23. 2.51	—	Admitted to hospital	—
OCTOBER-DECEMBER						
37	22.10.54	—	—	—	Transferred to another area	—
38	27.10.54	2. 5.55	July 1947	Continuing	—	37 10 0
39	2.11.54	Current	1.11.54	Continuing	—	—
40	15.11.54	4. 2.55	26. 7.54	5	—	65 0 0
41	27.11.54	7. 2.55	17. 9.48	1	—	62 10 0
						£1,614 0 0

December 1956 was 301. Out of these eighty-two cases were referred from the National Assistance Board, ninety-four from general practitioners and other medical specialists and the rest from a variety of sources from within the community; while a few were self-referrals. All cases referred had basically work problems as the presenting cause. With these larger referrals it was possible to understand a deeper significance of unemployment. It was not only a question of a job not being available but of increasing dissatisfaction as to the *nature* of work.

A study of these 301 cases shows that unemployment penetrates into the deepest areas of human personality. The onset of sudden unemployment may cause some depression with subsequent loss of interest in sexuality for example. During this period the unemployed man is recognisably in a state of anxiety, having nightmares and difficulties in sleeping. Having no outlet at all, in time a complete apathy establishes itself and in this state he becomes 'workshy'.

My tentative conclusion at that time was that all those who deal with employment problems need some ability to recognise those individuals who are emotionally disturbed as the result of unemployment or who are unemployed as a result of deep disappointment in work. I suggested that all those dealing with unemployment need to be aware of the emotional factors operating in people; these include general practitioners as well as all others in the employment field.

The training of social workers for psychiatric settings has been greatly influenced by the technique as well as the theory of psycho-analysis. While I respect this approach *per se*, I have not found that this type of technique is appropriate to the unemployed in the community; on the contrary, many people could only be induced to accept help provided this was offered in an informal and quasi-social manner. It is important, I said then (1958), that social workers should explore ways of helping just those people who, because they are unable to accept the relative impersonality of the formal interview, refuse help until the point of complete breakdown:

> 'We must be friends and teachers, listeners and talkers, lecturers and lectured-to, passive and often directive, understanding but at times even reproachful. We are part of the community, a new brand of specialists. . . . We are no appendix (to other professions) but professional workers, who may contribute something to the mental health of the nation in our own right with our own techniques and experience.'[2]

2. TOWARDS THE PRESENT

From 1958 onwards I carried on working with the unemployed. Roughly speaking 50 per cent were enabled to return to long-term employment, the other 50 per cent I could not help. By 1966 I had been able to identify five types of work problems. They fell into distinct categories and the correct 'treatment' depended to a considerable extent on their recognition.[3]

(*a*) There were those who were unemployed because of unrecognised or recognised emotional or mental illness

Individuals who fell into this first category had been considered 'sick', because of 'something significant that happened to them in their early past'. I now found that Man is not only the product of his past, but of his present. It was possible to have a normal childhood and still, through social circumstances, to become a problem. Therefore help offered to the unemployed would not only consist of 'digging up' the past, but *would also use the present as a satisfying experience to counteract the products of the past.*

(*b*) There were those who were unemployed for reasons beyond their control

I said in 1966:[3]

'There are the victims of automation, modernisation and of industrial closures. I cannot stress enough that this is one of the biggest problems of our time, and the problem about which industry must take action, or thousands of people will suffer unnecessary misery. Often breakdown begins, with rumours of a factory closing down.'

In 1966 I had enough evidence to say that the threat of change is the root cause of absenteeism. From all the work I had done so far, I saw this as the most urgent problem which needed to be tackled at a national level for both human and economic reasons. To mitigate the effects, I suggested that as soon as an industry knows it is going to close down, discussions should take place to decide on the best course of action for employees. But it was also evident that modern industry has claimed another set of victims: those who could no longer find any creative satisfaction in work. Into this I put the aimless youth and hooligans of our age. Having accumulated material now (by 1966 I had interviewed 1,200 unemployed) I saw that if nothing is done about these young people then we move into a very dangerous and violent society by the end of this century, when working hours will have been considerably reduced and people will have more leisure on their hands. I suggested that these young people must be given some creative outlet or interest outside the traditional model of work. The drifting youngsters of our society failed to respond to admonitions to return to work; but provided they had a real interest in *something*, they could usually be persuaded to enter work through this interest.

'Here the long-term remedy may lie in the educational system. At the moment it is designed almost exclusively to equip one for a job. Those who fail its course consider themselves total failures. But if the basic system were revised to include purposeful creative activities, many of our problems would be solved. A parallel situation can be found in the ancient Greek and Roman civilisations, where, because all the work was done by slaves, people had time on their hands. As a result quite ordinary people found an outlet in the creation of beautiful works of art. The modern do-it-yourself movement may well be a manifestation of the same need in our society.'[3]

(*c*) The High IQ Unemployed

This was a small and diminishing group of extremely intelligent men, who had missed the educational boat. As a result they had become embittered, frequently joined extremist political movements, so rationalising their bitterness, and had become cunning in avoiding work. Rehabilitation was a long and difficult task; the solution lay in accepting their intelligence and bitterness, finding them *training* for jobs (or alternative lifetasks) in which they could use their intelligence and derive satisfaction from their work.

(*d*) The Low IQ Unemployed

Quite frequently the low intelligence of this group was unrecognised, but they were generally capable of undertaking seasonal manual labour. Society, I felt, must resign itself to the fact that (until we find alternative lifetasks for them) they will have to live for periods off National Assistance.

(*e*) The Lazy

The real hard-core work-shy amounted to no more than 1 per cent of those with work problems.

3. TOWARDS THE FUTURE

There appears to be a two-way traffic from past to present and from present to past. The first one had been explored and expressed by the psycho-dynamic approach, but little, if anything, had been said about the latter. Not only does the past influence our present, but our present sense of satisfaction and frustration has an effect on the way we perceive the past. 'Man is not only what he was, but what he does, and what he does alters what he is.'[4]

The necessity to feel and to be useful is imperative to reinforce early patterns of security. On reflection after nearly thirty years of work with the unemployed I had to perceive that men and women of all ages *must* feel a sense of usefulness.

We must now recognise that industrial society has come to an end and we are entering a post-industrial society. Work, as we have known it since the industrial revolution, is over. A new technical revolution throws millions of people on the rubbish heap. Man needs to be active, needs to express his or her own particular personality in ways which are significant to his or her individual needs. But very few of those millions, who at present are facing a hopeless future, have any knowledge about their own capabilities and even less so of the translation of it into some lifetask. I use this expression to convey that the alternative to employment must be something other than work in the *traditional* sense. People still need to work, but the nature, volume and expression of their labour will have to be differently explored, expressed and used than hitherto. There are therefore three aspects that need consideration: exploration, expression and utilisation.

(*a*) Exploration

The tendency to blame governments for large-scale unemployment is myopic. The crisis of change is not limited to one or even a few countries in the world. Government's responsibility, however, individually and collectively, is still great, because they will have to consider the redistribution of funds at present going under the various names of public assistance, welfare, unemployment benefit or social security. It is totally unwise to allow people to remain useless. Such funds re-channelled through voluntary organisations would become the first step to introduce alternatives to employment. These funds, if properly used and distributed, would be instrumental in teaching teachers how to explore and develop in the young a sense of worth and help to develop their innate ability towards meaningful activity. Thus the young should be trained to enter a new arena of lifetask, not in the competitive fields of endeavour but in newly created private workshops and cottage industries. In time, as the present form of unemployment increases further, and less and less men and women are able to work in traditional work settings, it will become socially acceptable to practise lifeskills in a new way.

Exploration means that new methods and techniques are required by those who have educational and social responsibility. We are to see the emergence of a new type of social educators whose primary function will be to help the young (and not so young) to use themselves effectively.

During the last quarter century I slowly prepared myself and some of my colleagues and students for such new tasks. I evolved measurement techniques as well as instrumentation to evaluate on a scientific basis levels of satisfaction and frustration. (Tables II and III will give some idea of some early results of my Scale of Social Functioning.) During this work it became evident that we had greatly ignored in our educational and social approach the great potential that frustration may represent for creative endeavour.

Table II

Origin of Sample	No.	Average Total Score
Dr Barnardo's Homes	10	69·5/65·6
Controls	10	75·4/71·6
Family Service Unit	100	44·7/39·4
Mental Health Departments	74	50·9/45·1
Probation Service	50	47·2/38·9
Churchgoers	50	79·0/72·0
Non-churchgoers	44	79·0/73·5

Table III

Sample Area	Dr Barnardo's	Controls	Family Service	Mental Health	Probation Service	Churchgoers	Non-Churchgoers
Financial	14·0/12·8	12·0/11·6	6·2/4·5	8·6/ 7·5	8·5/ 6·1	15·0/14·0	13·6/12·8
Sexual	15·6/14·2	16·2/15·6	10·7/9·3	11·7/ 8·5	11·1/ 9·2	15·7/13·6	14·1/12·4
Primary Family	10·6/ 9·6	15·7/14·0	8·0/6·0	10·5/ 8·5	7·8/ 5·0	13·5/10·0	15·0/12·2
Secondary Family	16·5/16·0	15·3/13·7	11·0/9·7	13·6/13·0	12·0/10·0	20·0/20·0	19·0/18·5
Friendship	12·2/11·4	15·0/13·4	8·9/8·4	10·0/ 9·0	8·8/ 7·8	16·5/15·5	14·5/14·0
Work/ Interests	13·5/13·0	14·3/13·7	9·5/6·7	8·5/ 7·6	9·6/ 7·6	16·5/15·5	17·0/16·5

In order to understand the full significance of work we may have to reach back, in the first instance, to early childhood. First impressions of the world are implanted in our minds through the relationship between mother and child. Not only does our existence depend on this primary relationship, but also our first satisfactions. These areas of satisfaction are as follows:

(i) Security in relation to basic needs.
(ii) Sensual pleasure through being fed, caressed, cared for.
(iii) Non-sensual pleasure, i.e., mutual affection.
(iv) The basis of primary relationship: 'I am not alone, someone is with me.'
(v) Primitive play activities, at first directed mainly towards the mother and later towards toys.[5]

As the child grows older, these original satisfactions are also found in the outer world, and the ability to find them may depend on the quality of original experience.

(i) Security is now represented by income and comforts.
(ii) Sensual pleasure by intimate (sexual) relationships.
(iii) Mutual affection in the ability to love, i.e., grow through and with the partner in marriage and children.
(iv) Primary relationship through its extension to a circle of friends.
(v) Play activities in terms of meaningful or creative work and/or hobbies.

Thus society and all it can offer becomes as it were an extension of mother and continues what she started. But if she (society or mother) fails too massively, the individual's capacity to find these satisfactions is likely to be impaired.

It seems from all the work I had done that frustration, unless it is overwhelming (see basic standards in Tables II and III), is the spur for creative activities. (I do not use the word only in an artistic sense.) Those whose satisfactions level is below sixty cannot utilise their frustrations without active support.

Earlier I also said that we tended to see a one-way traffic from past to present. Now I can see that satisfactions, properly used and expressed, are 'sending back messages' to a somewhat frustrated childhood; that the damage in fact is being 'repaired'.

The exploration in children of the creative use of this frustration could bring about a vigorous and vital young generation that need not destroy others or themselves.

(*b*) Expression

The question can be raised, how is this change going to be in fact achieved? Who is going to do what, to help to develop a true expression of the personality? I referred to a new type of social educator, who may have a double function: to help the child across his schooling to get acquainted with himself and his true potentials, and to be instrumental in training teachers to enable them to take over this task as an extension of their teaching functions.

We live millions of experiences through our growing years and later, and only a few of us achieve a satisfying and meaningful existence by putting our experiences to proper use. The methods and techniques serve to help children (and others) *to make sense* of life's experiences. Many people see existence as a series of unconnected events, without significance. Our methods and techniques assist the young (and others) through a careful and disciplined psycho-social feedback system (and not interpretation) to make sense of life. This feedback of connected experiences eventually conveys to the individual that life is meaningful, because there is a purpose and possible utilisation in experiencing pain and pleasure.

(*c*) Utilisation

I spoke about exploration and expression; but when everything is said and done, who will benefit from these newly acquired skills?

Based on Christian principles going back for 2,000 years, and before that, to the Hebrew Laws regulating the conduct of the rich towards the poor (in ancient Israel and Judea part of the field after harvest had to be left for the poor, the sick and the widows), a feeling of compassion and care towards the weak in society had been slowly evolving, penetrating various social systems. The former Prime Minister of Britain, Mr Callaghan, not so long ago spoke of the need to establish a 'caring society'.

There are increasing numbers of old people who can ill afford the basic necessities, and go short of repairs, clothing and often specialised equipment (like orthopaedic shoes). There are also large numbers of people who are ill and helpless and have no energy to cater for their basic needs. A caring society should offer well trained people's services to them, from carpentry to tailoring, repairs and entertainment.

The training of the young and the re-training of the more mature will have a relevant double function: to give a new meaning to work, and the right to work on one hand; and to care for those who cannot afford to pay for basic services. The right to work is basic to every individual on this planet, but the right to exist without fear of being useless is imperative to the survival of our civilisation.

Notes

1. Eugene Heimler 'Psychiatric Social Work with National Assistance Board Cases' *The Medical Officer* 94 (16 December 1955) 351-353.
2. Eugene Heimler 'The Emotional Significance of Work' *The Medical Officer* 98 (16 August 1957) 96-98.
3. Joy Larkcom 'Beyond the Working Fringe' *Personnel Magazine* (June 1966).
4. Bruno Bettelheim *The Informed Heart* (London).
5. Eugene Heimler 'Looking Behind Cold Facts' *New Society* (18 April 1963).

Appendix

Table I

From Eugene Heimler 'Psychiatric Social Work with National Assistance Board Cases' *The Medical Officer* 94 (16 December 1955) 351-353.

Table II

In the article reference has been made to measurement of satisfaction and frustration. This instrument is known as the *Heimler Scale of Social Functioning*. In 1962 Dr Neville Davis, a general practitioner, and Eugene Heimler, a psychiatric social worker, assessed satisfaction levels on various population samples using this instrument. The maximum possible point is 100 in the total Scale and the maximum possible score in each particular area is twenty. The established norms for average total scores is between seventy-two and seventy-nine and the average norm in each sample area is twelve. Table II shows scores taken from various community groups, including an orphanage, Dr Barnardo's Homes, where the subjects were followed up thirty to forty-five years after they had left the orphanage. The average total scores refer to satisfaction levels obtained from the community and social services.

Reprinted from Neville Davis, LMSS (Lond.), MCGP and Eugene Heimler, AAPSW 'An Experiment in the Assessment of Social Function' *The Medical Officer* (20 January 1967).

Table III

Area sub-scores of various community groups. The norms are represented by the 'churchgoers' and 'non-churchgoers'.

Ibid, as to Table II.

B. The Right to Work

Ronald Krietemeyer

The Genesis and Development of the Right to Work

THE RIGHT to a decent job has been the basis for a broad range of efforts by governments, labour unions, and other social institutions to establish public policies that guarantee full employment. This essay will highlight some of the major developments in the attempt by western nations to recognise the right to a job through appropriate social and economic policies. I will use the experience of the United States as a starting point and will then contrast this to the approach of several European nations.

In public policy terms the right to a job relates directly to the issues of full employment and unemployment. Policies aimed at achieving full employment are the major way in which governments attempt to embody the right to a job in their social and economic systems. Much of this discussion, therefore, will centre around policies to achieve full employment.

Since the earliest days of mercantilism in the fifteenth century, unemployment has been a significant social concern. Until several centuries later, however, there was no explicit general concept of full employment policy. Relief of the unemployed poor consisted of either 'outdoor relief' or the workhouse—reflecting a general social antagonism to idleness. The economic growth of the factory system was promoted as the ultimate solution to unemployment.[1]

The concept of governmentally guaranteed work was first suggested in 1836 by Louis Blanc, a French historian. Michael Harrington has pointed out that the idea was tried in Paris during the Revolution of 1848, and until the ascendance of Marxism in the last part of the nineteenth century, this is what most Europeans understood to be socialism.[2]

Classical economists held that unemployment was only an accidental aberration. They denied the possibility of serious continuing unemployment in the competitive free enterprise system. In contrast to this view, Marx promoted the thesis that the creation of 'a reserve army of the unemployed' was an inherent feature of the capitalist system. By its very nature, he believed, the system has a chronic incapacity to achieve full employment.

The classical *laissez-faire* proposition, as stated by Adam Smith in the eighteenth century, held that as long as there is genuine competition in the economy, trade unions or government regulations, or any other form of conscious intervention is unnecessary because a free market actually regulates itself. So long as the decisions of businessmen were not distorted by trade unions or social legislation, competition in the economy would ensure a tendency towards full employment.

Changes throughout the western world in this fundamental view about the appropriate role of government in the economy were at the core of the twentieth-century attempts to achieve full employment and guarantee everyone the right to a decent job. Let us turn to look at the experience in the United States.

1. FULL EMPLOYMENT POLICY IN THE US

(*a*) The New Deal and The Second World War

The Great Depression brought about a virtual revolution in ideas and policy concerning unemployment. It was a crisis that shook America to its core. By 1932, more than 5,000 banks had failed, 86,000 businesses had gone bankrupt and investment and production virtually came to a halt. The result was massive unemployment. By 1933 one in every four workers was without a job.

President Franklin D. Roosevelt, in his first inaugural address on 4 March 1933, said: 'Our greatest primary task is to put people to work.' In his second Fireside Chat, on 30 September 1934, Roosevelt said: 'I stand or fall by my refusal to accept as a necessary condition of our future a permanent army of unemployed.' The New Deal programme of President Roosevelt led to large-scale job creation programmes funded by the government. In reaction to a massive economic crisis, the government was intervening in unprecedented ways in the national economy.

In 1936 the conceptual approach to unemployment was revolutionised by John Maynard Keynes' work, *The General Theory of Employment, Interest and Money*. Keynes fundamentally challenged the *laissez-faire* approach to full employment and built the case for government intervention to affect the levels of employment and unemployment. Public officials of the New Deal seized on Keynes' General Theory as the basis for activist interventions to reduce unemployment.

It was also during the 1930s that the trade union movement expanded very rapidly throughout America. The rapid spread of unionisation brought a deep change in the conditions of workers. The development of negotiated contracts with management established the principle that workers had certain basic rights. Wage and hour standards were developed, and fringe benefits such as pensions and health insurance added to the creation of an overall standard of economic security for the unionised worker. Above all, job security was considered to be the central role of the trade unions. The earliest contracts were often only one page long, and their central demand was most often for the establishment of a system of job security.

While public policies during the Great Depression and the New Deal represented a dramatic break from the classical *laissez-faire* approach to unemployment, still *full employment* was never an issue during this period. The economic crisis was so massive that the programmes enacted by the government were aimed only at reducing the extreme levels of unemployment, not at eliminating unemployment. As late as 1940 the official unemployment rate was about 15 per cent. Nevertheless, the New Deal programmes, while far from achieving full employment, were very significant because they demonstrated that large-scale government intervention through both public works and direct public employment is a realistic and effective way to create jobs and reduce the levels of unemployment.

Although the nature of the discussion about full employment changed significantly during the New Deal days, the political realities reflected an unwillingness to embody in public policy the right of all persons to a decent job. For example, in 1934 the National

Resources Planning Board (NRPB), an agency created by President Roosevelt, submitted a programme based on a 'New Bill of Rights'. It was entitled *Security, Work and Relief Policies*, and the first item was the 'right to work, usefully and creatively through the productive years'. The second item was 'the right to fair pay, adequate to command the necessities and amenities of life . . .'. At the core of this new programme was the assumption of strong, central government planning and a significant redistribution of social and economic resources. Three months after President Roosevelt submitted this report to Capitol Hill, Congress killed the National Resources Planning Board. In the months and years that followed, the conservative forces in Congress were able repeatedly to defeat the comprehensive planning for full employment that was the goal of President Roosevelt and Congressional liberals.

The definition of 'full employment' also became a stumbling block in the concrete attempts to implement this goal. President Roosevelt, in his 1944 annual address to Congress, set forth a 'Second Bill of Rights', the first of which was the 'right for all to . . . a useful and remunerative job in the industries or shops or farms or mines of the nation . . .'. He sought from Congress the support for the necessary government programmes to provide the sixty million jobs that were required to achieve full employment.

Others, however, did not agree with Roosevelt's comprehensive definition of full employment. Full employment was defined in a more restrictive sense by business leaders and more conservative political spokesmen of that period. They spoke of 'high employment', or 'as many jobs as we can', or 'a satisfactory high level of employment'.[3] While these leaders accepted the Keynesian-style government interventions that were necessary to prevent a return to Depression unemployment levels, they clearly did *not* accept a firm government commitment to literally guarantee every person a right to a job.

The Second World War led to an unprecedented increase in military investment and production in the US. Twelve million men and women were added to the armed services, and an additional eight million persons entered the labour force as a result of the production demands of the war. These factors virtually eliminated unemployment in the economy. In short, full employment was achieved as a result of the unique circumstances of a global war.

Full employment as a public policy goal took on much greater significance on the post-war economic agenda. In a discussion of this period, Herbert Stein writes:

> Full employment became the flag around which every one could rally. . . . Political leaders, government officials, and all private parties directly concerned with influencing economic policy came to give much higher priority to full employment in their own scale of national objectives for peacetime.[4]

(*b*) Employment Act of 1946

One of the most indicative events in the development of full employment policy in the United States was the Congressional debate and passage of the Employment Act of 1946. Contrary to widespread public perception, the passage of this Act was not a full-scale victory for full employment advocates. In fact, it was in many respects a major defeat. The original bill that was introduced was the Murray-Wagner Full Employment Bill. The objective as stated in the bill was 'a national policy and program for assuring continuing full employment'. It stated that the meaning of this objective was that 'all Americans able to work and seeking work have the right to useful, remunerative, regular, and full-time employment, and it is the policy of the United States to assure the existence at all times of sufficient employment opportunities to enable all Americans freely to exercise this right'. This bill was firmly opposed by Congressional conservatives and business leaders. In the end it was rejected in favour of a much weaker substitute.

The bill that was actually passed was called the Employment Act of 1946. Significantly, the word 'full' was deleted from the title, and the substance of the bill was much different. The final version referred to 'maximum employment, production, and purchasing power'. This was to be pursued 'in a manner calculated to foster and promote free competitive enterprise'. The Act established the Council of Economic Advisors and the Congressional Joint Economic Committee which were required to submit reports and recommend actions and legislation aimed at achieving the maximum employment.

While the passage of this Act represented an unquestionable rejection of the *laissez-faire* philosophy, the fact that it had been dramatically weakened signalled a clear unwillingness on the part of the US Congress to go so far as committing the government to guaranteeing jobs for all.[5]

For the last three decades the major mechanisms in US policy to reduce unemployment have been broad fiscal and monetary policies. These were essentially Keynesian methods for stimulating or retarding consumer spending and investment. More focused methods of actually guaranteeing full employment were consistently rejected. As the modern economy changed, it became increasingly difficult to keep unemployment and inflation down by means of the traditional fiscal and monetary approach. Many economists began to suggest that full employment was simply not a realistic goal because it could not be achieved without causing high inflation.

Meanwhile, the trade union movement continued to be the source of the strongest and most consistent objections to the abandonment of full employment as a legitimate goal of economic policy. In 1972, a spokesman for the AFL-CIO, the major federation of American trade unions, made labour's position clear:

> Full employment as organized labor views it means job opportunities at decent wages for all those who are able to work and seek employment. . . . Business spokesmen, academic economists, and political leaders should stop playing games with the economic and social objective of full employment. If their goal is a 5 per cent or 4 per cent unemployment rate they may have reason for such a choice, but their objective is not full employment.[6]

(*c*) Full Employment and Balanced Growth Act

In an attempt to develop more co-ordinated and focused policies to achieve full employment, a major piece of new legislation was introduced in 1974—the Humphrey-Hawkins Full Employment and Balanced Growth Act. The original bill declared that every American capable of working has 'the right to equal opportunities for useful paid employment at fair rates of compensation'. The bill provided for annual presidential reports which would estimate the levels of employment, consumption and investment and would recommend actions that were necessary to achieve full employment. Among the various provisions of the bill was one which stated that anyone who had been deprived of the right to gainful employment could bring suit in federal court in order to seek redress. This constituted, in effect, a job guarantee with specific and legally enforceable assurances of gainful employment for all who were willing and able to work.

The history of this legislation is instructive in that it demonstrates the state of the full employment debate in recent US history. Most significant in this legislative history is that the bill was soon revised to exclude the judicial enforcement powers. In place of the 'job guarantee' that was in the original bill, a numerical goal of 3 per cent adult unemployment was established. Provisions were also added dealing with anti-inflation policies. With the strong support of the labour movement and a broad coalition of civil rights, religious and public interest organisations, the Full Employment and Balanced Growth Act was finally passed. Although the bill had been greatly weakened, it nevertheless set in place a mechanism that would allow for a new approach to economic policy. It explicitly recognised that 'aggregate monetary and fiscal policy have been unable to achieve full employment' and it required the President to state the government's economic goals and priorities and the policies it proposed to achieve them.

In the years since the passage of this Act, it has been increasingly ignored. Although it provides the framework for co-ordinated economic policy planning to achieve full employment, it has not been used effectively towards this end. Indeed, with the arrival of the current Administration, the requirements of the Act have been almost totally ignored and the government has moved even further away from a commitment to full employment. The right to a job remains a general principle rather than a concrete reality in American economic policy.

2. FULL EMPLOYMENT POLICY IN EUROPE

Western European countries were affected by some of the same major events that influenced the full employment debate in the US—the Great Depression, Second World War, and the post-war boom. Yet in very important ways, their purpose with respect to full employment policies has been quite different. This is particularly true in terms of their willingness to adopt a more coherent rationale for active government policies and social legislation aimed at ensuring jobs for all. The experiences of these nations are briefly examined below.[7]

(*a*) Sweden

Full employment is the central goal of Swedish economic policy. As former Prime Minister Olaf Palme stated in 1977:

> Full employment is the pillar of Swedish social policy. . . . It starts as a concept of work, not as the sociologists of the Fifties saw it, as a necessary evil from which to escape to leisure time where the important things in life took place, but as part of being human.[8]

Sweden's economy is heavily influenced by the trade union movement, not only because trade union economists were the intellectual source of the major innovations in Sweden's post-war economic policy. This is particularly true in that Swedish policies were based on a trade union conception of full employment rather than on the neoclassical or Keynesian conception of the goal. Keynesian economics is largely about [the overall rate of] employment while Swedish economics has more and more emphasised economic security, which is a deeper and much more extensive concept.[9]

In Swedish social policy, employment has been viewed as one of a set of basic human rights that must be guaranteed by society. Employment, education, health, and housing are considered so basic that they cannot be left to the workings of the free market. In the case of employment, the post-war economic approach in Sweden was based on the assumption that fiscal and monetary policy were inadequate for achieving genuine full employment. Instead, what was necessary was a series of policies to co-ordinate investment and the available labour force. This required not retraining, relocation, and temporary public employment programmes for unemployed workers, but also policies to stabilise private investment and limit layoffs during recessions. An independent agency called the Swedish Labour Market Board, jointly administered by business and the trade unions, was created to achieve these objectives.

In general, while the Swedish experience was not without its economic problems, it did serve to demonstrate that it was possible to achieve genuine full employment without unleashing massive inflation.

(*b*) Germany

While the German approach to overall economic policy was quite different from that of Sweden, it was similar in two important respects—it included an important and active role for trade unions, and a more co-ordinated system of economic planning than was accepted in the United States. The federation of German trade unions that was formed in 1948 endorsed a basic programme that included among its goals 'full employment', 'co-determination in all personal, social and economic questions arising in the management and design of the economy', and 'social justice' that was based on 'an equitable share for workers in the total returns of the economy'.

In many respects trade unions played a more extensive role in the German economy than in any other European country in the post-war period. One clear example of this was the 1951 law on co-determination, which reserved one-third of the seats on the board of directors of all large corporations for elected representatives of the firm's employees. Trade unions also play a central role in German manpower policy. They operate over 100 vocational training schools, and the major organisations for labour market policies is an independent agency run by labour and management.

Post-war industrial growth in Germany was highly co-ordinated and planned, although not directly by the government. It was largely the concentrated financial system, and especially the active role that the representatives of the German banks played in the management of specific companies that provided this co-ordination. Economic policymakers tended to move well beyond the traditional Keynesian approach in their willingness to intervene in the market for the purpose of achieving social goals such as full employment.

(*c*) Britain

Despite the public perception of Britain having instituted certain socialist policies in the post-war period, this nation's overall approach to economic policy and full employment was more similar to that of the United States than any other major European country. The one action in Britain that constituted a major rejection of the conventional American view was the nationalisation of several major industries. Yet these nationalised industries were never systematically co-ordinated or given a coherent set of goals.

There was in Britain, as in America, a general absence of active national policy in regard to long-term investment. After the Second World War, with the British Empire in decline, the traditional areas of investment were no longer as profitable. To maintain a high rate of economic growth and provide full employment, Britain needed a major effort to retool and modernise its industry. Without specific investment and planning policies, this did not occur.

The status of trade unions in Britain was perhaps more hostile to the managers and owners of capital than in any other western nation. The kind of social contracts and participation in employment policies that developed in Germany and Sweden were simply not possible in the British context. One reason for this was the structure of the

British trade union movement itself. In contrast to the sixteen unions in the German federation and the 128 unions in the AFL-CIO, there were 574 unions in Britain. Only 170 of these were affiliated with the British labour federation.

While full employment has been a goal for the labour unions and the Labour Party in Britain, national economic policies have not reflected sustained success in moving towards this goal. These policies have been largely restricted to conventional fiscal and monetary actions. Moreover, under the current Conservative government, Britain's policies have returned to many *laissez-faire* policies. As unemployment has increased, Britain along with the United States, has moved in recent years not closer but farther away from embodying the right to a job in public policy.

CONCLUSION

Several general conclusions can be drawn from this selective review of the development of the right to employment as reflected in public policy. It is clear, first of all, that the status of the trade union movements in western nations has been a key element in determining the extent to which full employment goals have been built into public policy. Secondly, the degree to which co-ordinated and long-term economic planning is an accepted part of a nation's policies greatly affects their ability to achieve full employment. Although western nations in the post-war era have increasingly adopted general policy goals of full employment, the enactment into law of a firm guarantee of employment for all has been much more difficult to achieve.

Notes

1. Joseph Schumpeter *History of Economic Analysis* (New York 1954) pp. 270 ff.
2. Michael Harrington 'Government Should Be The Employer of *First* Resort' *The New York Times Magazine* (26 March 1972) 44.
3. Herbert Stein *The Fiscal Revolution in America* (Chicago 1969) pp. 185-186.
4. Stein, *ibid.*, pp. 170 ff.
5. For an extensive treatment of the legislative history of the Employment Act of 1946, see Stephen K. Bailey *Congress Makes a Law: The Story Behind the Employment Act of 1946* (New York 1950).
6. Nat Goldfinger 'Full Employment: The Neglected Policy' *AFL-CIO American Federationist* (November 1973) pp. 7 and 9.
7. A more detailed analysis of the European experience is presented in Andrew Levison *The Full Employment Alternative* (New York 1980) pp. 105-154.
8. 'Palme' *New Yorker* 22 (June 1976) 22.
9. F. E. Banks 'Swedish Economic Policy: Some Current Problems' *Intereconomics* No. 12 (1974) 371.

International Labour Organisation, Geneva

Report VI (1) for the International Conference on Work 1983: Policies of Employment in the World

THE EMPLOYMENT Policy Convention (No. 122) and Recommendation (No. 122) of 1964 do not contain any provisions relating specifically to the right to work. The participants in the 1964 Session of the International Labour Conference quite obviously had this in mind, however, when they decided to refer in the Preamble to the Declaration of Philadelphia of the ILO ('all human beings, irrespective of race, creed or sex, have the right to pursue both their material well-being and their spiritual development in conditions of freedom and dignity, of economic security and equal opportunity') and to the Universal Declaration of Human Rights ('everyone has the right to work, to free choice of employment, to just and favourable conditions of work and to protection against unemployment'). Moreover, the references in the operative part (article 1, paragraphs 1 and 2) to the declaration and pursuit by each Member as a major goal of 'an active policy designed to promote full . . . employment' and the need for the said policy to aim at ensuring 'that there is work for all who are available for and seeking work' were presumably considered by those who drafted the text as a means of ensuring the right to work recognised in the Preamble of both instruments.

This interpretation has long gone unchallenged and there has been no indication on the part of the member States of any need for a more explicit statement in favour of the right to work. It is significant that the 1976 World Employment Conference, which recommended both the ratification of Convention No. 122 and its revision (Programme of Action, paragraphs 9 (*a*) and 33), makes no reference to the subject and that it was not until the 1979 Session of the International Labour Conference, in connection with the follow-up to the World Employment Conference, that the Director-General's attention was drawn, for the purpose of preparing the revision of the instruments, to article 23 of the Universal Declaration of Human Rights, to which reference has already been made, and to article 6 of the United Nations International Covenant on Economic, Social and Cultural Rights and article 6 of the United Nations Declaration on Social Progress and Development, both of which mention the recognition and guarantee of the right to work (see the resolution concerning the follow-up to the World Employment Conference, Part IV (*b*) (ii)).

In some thirty countries—20 per cent of the membership of the ILO and almost half of the States that have ratified Convention No. 122—the right to work is embodied in the constitution, national charter or other basic legislation. A comparative analysis of existing texts shows that there are three types of situation, according to whether they are found in socialist and developing countries with centrally planned economies, developing market-economy countries or industrialised market-economy countries.

The first group includes Algeria, Bulgaria, Byelorussian SSR, China, Cuba, Czechoslovakia, German Democratic Republic, Hungary, Mongolia, Poland, Romania, Ukrainian SSR, USSR and Yugoslavia.

In the second group, there are fourteen countries: Benin, Cape Verde, Colombia, Congo, Ecuador, India, Madagascar, Mexico, Peru, Philippines, Rwanda, Syrian Arab Republic, United Arab Emirates and Upper Volta.

The third group includes only Portugal and Spain.

The relevant texts contain various stipulations:

(1) as to the relationship between the right to work and the duty to collaborate in national production, economic development and the improvement of society: in the countries of the first group, it is the socialist principle of 'from each according to his ability, to each according to his work' that applies; and
(2) as to the guarantee or application of this right: the countries of the first group are the most explicit in this respect, since they state that 'the right [to work] is ensured by the socialist economic system, steady growth of the productive forces, free vocational and professional training, improvement of skills, training in new trades or professions, and development of the systems of vocational guidance and job placement' (Byelorussian SSR, Ukrainian SSR, USSR), or 'that the right to work . . . is guaranteed by the entire socialist economic system, to which economic crises and employment are unknown' (Czechoslovakia); for Portugal 'it shall be the responsibility of the State to guarantee the right to work by applying economic and social policies, and to ensure (*a*) the execution of full employment policies and the right to material assistance of persons who are unemployed against their will; (*b*) job security . . .; (*c*) equality of opportunity . . .'.

In addition, over sixty countries in various parts of the world, at different levels of development and having different economic, social and political systems, have adhered to the International Covenant on Economic, Social and Cultural Rights, whose article 6 provides for the right to work. Since the entry into force of the Covenant on 3 January 1976, the application of the right to work and other provisions it contains is subject to the supervisory procedures established by the Covenant itself. These procedures involve the submission of reports by the States and their consideration by the United Nations Economic and Social Council. The United Nations specialised agencies—and specifically the ILO—receive copies of these reports and are requested, in accordance with article 18 of the Covenant, to inform the Economic and Social Council of the progress made in achieving the observance of the provisions of the Covenant falling within the scope of their activities. Following a decision adopted by the Governing Body of the ILO in November 1976, the Committee of Experts on the Application of Conventions and Recommendations subsequently examined the measures adopted and the progress made by some thirty countries in the implementation, *inter alia*, of the article dealing with the right to work, on the basis of the government reports. The Committee's analysis and findings have been communicated to the United Nations and included in three reports published by the latter.

1. TRIPARTITE PARTICIPATION

Convention and Recommendation No. 122 lay down the principle of the participation of the social partners in terms which, without being identical, are very similar. The main references to the principle are found in article 3 of the Convention and paragraph 3 of the Recommendation (see texts attached).

Although these provisions refer to 'representatives of the persons affected' and make a distinction between 'representatives of employers and workers' and 'their organisations', the spirit of the texts presumably reflects a desire that there should be broad participation that is not restricted to the formally constituted employers' and trade union organisations.

This broad interpretation is based on two arguments:

(1) Whereas the Consultation (Industrial and National Levels) Recommendation, 1960 (No. 113), to which Recommendation No. 122 refers, speaks only of employers' and workers' organisations, Convention No. 141 and Recommendation No. 149, both of which were adopted in 1975 dealing specifically with rural workers' organisations—including both self-employed workers and wage earners—and their role in economic and social development, have since been interpreted by the ILO's Advisory Committee on Rural Development as applying to all types of rural workers' organisations, whether formally constituted or not. Such organisations therefore include agricultural wage earners' trade unions, co-operatives, community development groups, self-help groupings, charitable organisations, traditional groupings, etc.[1]

(2) In the present state of labour-management relations in non-industrialised countries, only 15 per cent of the labour force can be considered as being involved in a relationship in which the worker has a genuine or potential say in matters (compared to 85 per cent in the industrialised market-economy countries of Europe, North America and Japan).[2] It would therefore be contrary to ILO thinking to limit participation in the formulation of economic and social policies—including employment policies—to organised workers in the urban modern sector alone, particularly in the Third World, and not to endeavour to extend such participation as far as possible.

For these reasons it is possible and legitimate to consider participation, as it relates to these instruments, in the broadest sense. In practice, however, the member States do not yet take the same view and, generally speaking, make provision for the participation only of the most representative employers' and workers' organisations.

If the degree of effective participation were assessed only on the basis of the reports on ratified Conventions, submitted in accordance with article 22 of the ILO Constitution, it would appear minimal. Few of the reports presented in connection with preparations for the Office report on the application of Convention No. 122 refer to any procedure for the participation of the social partners. Only Sweden has a tripartite committee which, since 1977, has been advising the Government on matters connected with the drafting of reports for submission to the ILO on the application of ratified Conventions.

However, this does not take account of the real situation as regards participation by the social partners in the formulation and implementation of economic and social development policies. As long ago as 1973, an ILO survey[3] of thirty-three member countries listed over 100 examples of employers' and workers' participation in planning councils, committees, and similar bodies, both at the central level and at the sectoral, regional and local level. It is not always possible to distinguish clearly which of these institutions, whose numbers have since increased with the setting up of other participatory bodies, deal specifically with employment policies, though their terms of reference are often broad enough to suggest that they in fact do so. There is in any case no doubt about the matter in the case of bodies whose title refers to labour, employment, manpower or human resources, as in Australia, Austria, Bangladesh, Belgium, Botswana, Brazil, Chile, Colombia, Finland, France, India, Israel, Italy, Mexico, Netherlands, Nigeria, Pakistan, Panama, Peru, Philippines, Portugal, Sweden, Tunisia, United Kingdom and United States. In these bodies the 'horizontal' nature of the problem, i.e., the need for consistency between sectors, permits of an exchange of views between several ministerial departments, including the Planning and Labour ministries, on the one hand, and the employers' and workers' organisations, on the other.

The actual nature of the participation process is another matter. Convention No. 122 refers successively, in the same Article, to consultation concerning employment policies, co-operation in their formulation and support for their implementation; Recommendation No. 122, for its part, speaks of consultation in formulating the policies and co-operation in their implementation. Theoretically, several levels of participation are possible, from assistance in compiling data and the expression of points of view to co-determination and joint management. Here again, participation rarely seems to get beyond the first level, and employers' and trade union organisations may well be torn between a desire to influence government decisions and a concern not to appear committed to them, so as to 'underline the fact that their participation should be interpreted rather as an attempt to put their case than as evidence of their support'.[4] In order to judge the exact scope of the concepts of 'co-operation' and 'support' appearing both in article 3 of the Convention and in paragraph 3 of the Recommendation, it would perhaps be more relevant to examine more recent and more comprehensive information on the attitude of each of the social partners.

2. COLLECTIVE BARGAINING

There is another, even more direct, way for employers and workers to participate. This is collective bargaining which, from the standpoint of employment promotion and basic-needs satisfaction involves following up the national plan and going beyond existing legislation and which includes all forms of consultation between employers and wage earners, not just to resolve labour disputes but also to reconcile the interests and aspirations of the social partners.

It may seem surprising that collective bargaining is nowhere mentioned in Convention and Recommendation No. 122 as one of the means of concluding agreements on the promotion and protection of employment (except for the very general reference in paragraph 29 (1) of the Recommendation). This has several advantages, however: its flexibility (the social partners themselves decide what subjects to discuss), its realism (the measures agreed upon reconcile the desires of one side with the possibilities of the other), its precision (an agreement may cover an enterprise, a branch or more), and its effectiveness (stable employment derives from the consent of those who are expected to abide by the agreement, whatever form it takes). Moreover, under this system the social partners can act not just as economic agents that the public authorities inform or consult but as the actual instigators of supplementary employment policy measures for which they assume responsibility.

For all these reasons, collective bargaining has proved itself to be particularly effective in the fight against unemployment, especially in industrialised countries suffering from the current recession. The following are some examples.

(a) Right to information

In Italy, the collective agreements for the metal, chemical, construction and textile industries and for banks and commerce, which were renewed in 1979, stipulate that the enterprises shall inform the trade unions of investment plans and their effect on employment, the criteria for the location of plants, reorganisation and merger plans, etc. The situation is much the same in Spain, where a 1980 framework agreement lays down guidelines for the renewal of some 3,000 existing collective agreements.

(b) Job creation

The tripartite national agreement of Ireland and the metal industries agreement of the Netherlands contain a commitment to examine jointly measures to increase employment; in Italy, the Fiat and Olivetti agreements give the relevant figures for the targets set.

(c) Protection of employment

A guarantee to maintain employment at its present level, if necessary with the help of public funds appears in the iron and steel agreements of Luxembourg, the merchant navy agreement of Norway and in a job security plan for the dockers of thirty-four ports in the United States.

(d) Closure of enterprise

The aluminium industry collective agreement of the United States provides for better protection against dismissal; in Belgium, the decision to close an automobile plant was cancelled by agreement between the management and trade unions; an agreement on the closure of enterprises is annexed to the metal industries agreement in Switzerland.

(e) Rationalisation and reorganisation

In the Federal Republic of Germany half the labour force was estimated in 1974 to be protected under a collective agreement in the event of rationalisation plans; recently the Tuborg-Carlsberg enterprises in Denmark guaranteed job security during a rationalisation phase lasting up to 1985.

(f) Rescue plans

In Belgium, an interoccupational agreement was signed in 1975 on the revision of the concept of collective dismissal; more ambitious plans have been adopted for the revival of the iron and steel industry in France and the electronics industry in the Federal Republic of Germany, including such provisions as early retirement, guaranteed resources and social security, separation grants, etc.

(g) Reduction of hours

Work sharing as a means of protecting jobs is the main subject of collective bargaining conducted in several sectors in Belgium and in the automobile and aeronautics industries in the United States; in Spain, the employers and workers have agreed to submit a proposal to the Government aimed at lowering the legal age of retirement; in Belgium an interoccupational agreement exists on the supervision of overtime.

(h) Protection of specific categories

The Federal Republic of Germany has created an emergency fund under joint management to assist workers who have been dismissed; similarly, most older workers are covered by agreements providing for protection against dismissal and/or guaranteed wages; in Mexico, an agreement has been signed under which half the temporary workers in an automobile company have been given permanent status; in India the employment of apprentices in spinning mills is governed by an agreement.

(i) Basic needs of workers in an enterprise

The satisfaction of these can also be indirectly but definitely influenced by collective agreements. Collective agreements on social facilities and personnel benefits as regards the purchase of food, health, housing, training and transport can have a direct bearing on both the quality and the quantity of employment, by giving rise to new activities in the enterprise (safety and health units, company stores, canteens, etc.) and in the corresponding public and private services.

(ILO—Publications, CH-1211 Geneva 22, Switzerland. 1st ed. 1982, pp 9-16.

Notes

1 ILO *Rural employers' and workers' organisations and participation.* Advisory Committee on Rural Development, Ninth Session, Geneva, 27 Nov.-6 Dec. 1979, document ACRD IX/1979/III (Geneva 1979) pp. 16-19.

2 These percentages are based on Guy Caire *Freedom of association and economic development* (Geneva, ILO, 1976) table 1, pp. 8-9.

3 ILO *Employers' and workers' participation in planning* (Geneva 1973) pp. 231-239.

4 Jean-Jacques Bonnaud 'Participation by workers' and employers' organisations in planning in France' in *International Labour Review* (Geneva, ILO) Apr. 1966, p. 360.

Friedhelm Hengsbach

The Church and the Right to Work

BEFORE THE Second Vatican Council the question of the right to work would probably have been given an exhaustive answer. Either systematic recourse would have been had to some form of Catholic social teaching in order to deduce concrete prescriptions for action from general premisses, or certain passages from papal doctrinal statements that proclaimed this fundamental right would have been adduced. However, the view of the Church's social teaching that is expressed in Vatican II's pastoral constitution on the Church in the world of today decided against the kind of social teaching that had developed in the German-speaking world, a philosophical and rational approach basing its arguments on the natural law, and decided in favour of a biblical and pastoral approach responding to the actual context of people's lives. This latter approach had long been practised in the French-speaking world under the motto: 'See, judge, act'. In an analogous fashion I shall now present campaigns undertaken or supported by the Church, views put forward in Church documents, considerations of social ethics and political consequences.

1. CAMPAIGNS

In the winter of 1975-76 the Speyer branch of the Vereinigte Flugtechnische Werke (VWF) was threatened with closure and the sacking of some thousand workers. As news of the management's plans leaked out, Church organisations like the Catholic Workers' Movement (KAB) and the Young Christian Workers (YCW) expressed their solidarity with the workers affected. They mobilised the local inhabitants and the Church leadership and organised demonstrations and meetings. Ultimately the pressure of public opinion on the trade unions, political parties and the firm's management became so strong that the original decision was reconsidered and the works council was assured that the jobs would be kept.

The new experience that 'the Churches are on our side', the experience of local parishes, Church organisations, deaneries and bishops expressing their solidarity with works councils and trade unions, has been repeated many times since Speyer, as the workers concerned have resisted plant closures said to be unavoidable on economic grounds, often learning the news first from the press, radio or television, and have gone on to demand the right to work. Examples have been a textile company in Mönchengladbach in January 1980, a Hoesch subsidiary at Krefeld in February 1980, van Delden at Gronau in March 1981, Adler-Triumph at Frankfurt in June 1981, Videocolor at Ulm in January 1982, Vereinigte Glaswerken (VEGLA) near Aachen in March 1982, and Deutz-Magirus in April 1982.[1]

Employers' organisations were at first very uncertain about how to react to this kind of public opposition. Later their objective became confidential talks with the Church leadership with only a few people taking part. They wanted the Church as an institution to remain predictable and to remember its proper role of pastoral care and of salvation transcending death, as well as the possibilities of making some kind of comprehensive sense of life in a pluralist society. Economic expertise was not in their view something the Church could lay claim to.[2] The normal response of Church spokesmen was that individual economic decisions of a particular management could not be treated in isolation from the total economic context and that they should rather respect the limitations of the economic, social and political framework within which they were made and should acknowledge a comprehensive ethical stance. The churches and especially Church organisations in this field, as part of the labour movement, would take the side of the workers affected and try to safeguard their skills and importance whenever what was at stake was the well-being of the individual and the interest of society as a whole.

2. ATTITUDES

In the Church's social teaching there are three lines of approach that postulate a right to work.

(a) The Right to Work and the Right to Sustenance

Pope Leo XIII distinguished between the personal character of work, to the extent that the exertion of work springs from the personal decision of the person doing it, and its character of necessity, to the extent that it must provide the worker with sustenance. Although the argument is directed immediately towards the level of wages, which should not be left to the discretion of the partners to the contract, given the inequality of the positions from which they are negotiating, but should be determined by the necessity of maintaining life, it does not lose its logic when applied to a right to work: 'The preservation of life is the bounden duty of one and all . . . It necessarily follows that each one has a natural right to procure what is required in order to live; and the poor can procure that in no other way than by what they can earn through their work.'[3]

Pius XII did indeed confirm, with reference to Leo XIII, the connection between work and sustenance, but at the same time he placed in the background the situation of the dependent worker and the special character of the relationship of wage-labour. The result of this nuanced treatment was to give prominence to a right to work seen as an aspect of freedom: 'The maintenance of life is, however, a strict personal duty that is imposed by nature. The personal duty of working imposed by nature is a consequence of the personal duty imposed by nature to provide for one's own life and that of one's dependents by work. Hence the commandment of nature is ordered towards the sublime goal of man's sustenance. But it must be observed that this duty and the right to work that corresponds to it derive primarily from nature and not from society, as if man were nothing but someone delegated by society to work.'[4]

The Second Vatican Council deduced from the dignity of the human person an undifferentiated series of fundamental rights: 'Therefore, there must be made available to all men everything necessary for leading a life truly human, such as food, clothing, and shelter; the right to choose a state of life freely and to found a family, the right to education, to employment, to a good reputation, to respect, to appropriate information. . . .[5]

(b) The Right to Work and the Value of Work in Itself

The Second Vatican Council stressed the precedence of work over all other factors of economic life, which it saw as being purely instrumental. Work is the immediate expression of the human personality, a participation in God's creative activity, an association with Jesus the worker. 'From all these considerations there arise every man's duty to labour faithfully and also his right to work.'[6]

Pope John Paul II has conceived of work as a source of the rights of the working person himself or herself, rights which must be seen in the larger context of human rights as a whole. The human rights that arise from work result from the multifarious nature of man's duty to work, 'both because the Creator has commanded it and because of his own humanity, which requires work in order to be maintained and developed. Man must work out of regard for others, especially his own family, but also for the society he belongs to, the country of which he is a child, and the whole human family of which he is a member, since he is the heir to the work of generations and at the same time a sharer in building the future of those who will come after him in the succession of history.'[7]

(c) The Right to Work and the Social Organisation of Work

Influenced by the mass unemployment of his day that was a consequence of the world-wide economic crisis, Pius XI reminded those taking part in negotiations about wages of their responsibility for the economy as a whole, something they could not evade in fixing the level of wages: 'Another point . . . of scarcely less importance must not be overlooked, in these our days especially, namely that opportunities for work be provided for those who are willing and able to work.'[8] Pius XII ascribed primarily to the two sides of industry the task of regulating the conditions of work: it was only if they could not fulfil this task that the State should intervene in creating and distributing jobs.[9] John XXIII reminded the State of the duty of creating the conditions in which individual men and women were genuinely able to claim their personal rights, and of guaranteeing social alongside economic progress. 'The government is also required to show no less energy and efficiency in the matter of providing opportunities for suitable employment, graded to the capacity of the workers.'[10] The Second Vatican Council laid a similar duty on society: 'It is the duty of society, moreover, according to the circumstances prevailing in it, and in keeping with its proper role, to help its citizens find opportunities for adequate employment.'[11]

John Paul II has discussed in detail the present social interdependence and organisation of work, in other words the legal relationship of the dependent employee and the direct and indirect employer.[12] A 'fundamental right of everyone to work' may be only formulated incidentally, but it is unequivocally presented as a genuine duty on the part of the indirect employer. While the direct employer is responsible for the actual conditions of work and subscribes to the contract of work, the indirect employer includes 'both persons and institutions of various kinds, and also collective labour contracts and the *principles* of conduct which are laid down by these persons and institutions and which determine the whole socio-economic *system* or are its results'.[13] If one wanted to pin an institutional label on the indirect employer, then the names one would cite would be governments, central banks, trade unions, employers' organisations, the International Monetary Fund, the General Agreement on Tariffs and Trade (GATT). Among these 'agents at the national and international level that are responsible for the whole orientation of labour policy'[14] the encyclical mentions first of all the State. But since the age of self-sufficient nation States is past, the world economic system as an intricate complex of relationships of mutual dependence has developed into the role of the indirect employer. At the same time the existing one-sided relationships of domination and dependence that characterise this system have the evil effect of maintaining the unequal exchange of finished goods and raw materials, of increasing the disparity in income between industrialised and developing countries, and of making, even worse the extreme misery of working people in the economically disadvantaged developing countries. The indirect employer's overriding duty is 'the question of finding work, or, in other words, the issue of *suitable employment for all who are capable of it*. The opposite of a just and right situation in this field is unemployment, that is to say the lack of work for those who are capable of it. It can be a question of general unemployment in certain sectors of work. The role of the agents included under the title of indirect employer is *to act against unemployment*, which in all cases is an evil, and which, when it reaches a certain level, can become a real social disaster.'[15]

3. REFLECTIONS

The aim of the reflections that follow is to consider in greater depth the threefold pattern of reasons for a right to work: the comprehensive valuation of human work, the legal guarantee of formal and real freedom, and the class situation of workers that results from the social conflict between labour and capital.

(a) Aspects of the value of human work

Statements by the Church's teaching authority provide a material reason for the right to work by reference to ensuring one's livelihood and a personal reason by reference to man's realisation of his own potentialities. The apparent ambiguity is an indistinct reflection of the evaluation of human work that characterises the Judaeo-Christian tradition. The biblical evaluation of work in fact disowns the division of man that was linked with the old view of human work which differentiated between work and leisure, manual and intellectual work, man's work and woman's work, and which finally saw man at work as the rival of the gods. Judaism and Christianity saw work as service to God, as the expression of the fundamental equality of all men in the sight of this God. Hence they respected every form of human activity as an actual symbol of God's creative power.

Three aspects of the value of human work can be traced in the Church's social teaching. Human work has a natural and human dimension. It serves man's physical survival in a fundamentally hostile world. Man must win his daily bread in the struggle for existence, in the continual battle with nature. This struggle took on harsh traits of alienation in man's primitive history. But in contrast to this condition of being at nature's mercy, man today seems to be capable of extreme violence against nature, of which he forms a part. Hence the first aspect of human work is gaining one's livelihood in agreement with nature.

Beyond this, human work has a personal dimension. It serves man's self-expression. Work is a good thing for man 'because through work man *not only transforms nature*, adapting it to his own needs, but he also *achieves fulfilment* as a human being and indeed, in a sense, becomes "more a human being"'.[16] Work emerges from man and is directed to man. The result of work and the process of work cannot be separated from the worker. Each sort of work 'is judged above all by *the measure of the dignity* of the subject of work, that is to say the person, *the individual who carries it out*'.[17] Self-expression is the second aspect of human work.

Finally, human work has a social dimension. People's different gifts and interests tend towards the social organisation of work. Moreover, man does not find his fulfilment in isolation but is dependent on social recognition. 'Further, when work is done in common, when hope, hardship, ambition and joy are shared, it brings together and firmly unites the wills, minds and hearts of men: in its accomplishment, men find themselves to be brothers.'[18] Establishing one's position in society is the third aspect of human work.

These three aspects modify the content of the claim to a right to work. In the first place, a right to work would be very problematical if it could only be guaranteed at the cost of an artifical increase in consumption or the progressive commercialisation of what had hitherto been private dimensions of life or the further destruction of the environment. Secondly, a right to work that is suitable for men needs to correct both the capitalist's interests in a return on his capital with its restriction to the short term and to a single trade or industry as well as the worker's predominant preference for income so that they are often ready to accept burdensome and unhealthy conditions of work such as piecework, overtime, night-shifts and flexible rostering in the illusory expectation of being able to compensate themselves for this by a greater income and greater consumption in their leisure time. And in the third place a fundamental right to work for every human being within the conditions imposed by the limitations of the world's environment and capacity for growth would be irreconcilable with the aggressive export policies adopted by many industrial nations, which unload their products and processes on the Third World in order to ensure their own jobs but which make only a tiny contribution towards solving the food and employment problems of precisely the poorer developing nations. But it would also be irreconcilable with the widespread agreement of trade unions in the industrialised nations to tariff barriers, import controls and one-sided treaties aimed at the alleged competition of the developing countries. Even if workers' solidarity is not very well developed at the national and international level, it will not wait until it can re-distribute the increase in production and the increase in jobs that goes with it but will already approve of an equal and fair re-distribution of the growth in productivity even when the level of production remains the same, so that the work available would be shared between those in employment and the unemployed, between men and women, between adults and young people, between the industrialised and the developing nations, between the present and the future generation.

(b) Formal and real freedom

Whether consciously or unconsciously, the statements by the Church's teaching authority on the right to work leave undecided whether what they are concerned to proclaim and justify is a fundamental right of freedom or a fundamental social right. This lack of precision is excusable because the Church's social teaching had first to overcome previous judgments based both on a seventeenth-century view of society and on the subsequent liberal view until its view of the social reality of industrial society had come into focus. But when dealing with the question itself it was quick to take up positions that were clearly in opposition to the liberal conception of society.

The lack of understanding with regard to fundamental rights displayed by the liberal theory of society and the State is illustrated by a remark made by the former German Federal President Heuss. When the Assembly of the Länder was discussing the inclusion of a right to work in the constitution he wondered whether there ought not to be a constitutional guarantee of a right to idleness too.

The rejection of fundamental social rights is merely consistent with the liberal understanding of the constitution. Liberal economic theory originally assumed that the individual had complete freedom to decide on his economic activity, that he freely chose the occupation that corresponded to his capabilities and inclinations, and that he took sole responsibility for insurance for the future and the education of his children. On this view a person's income, chances of promotion and position in the social pecking order are exclusively the result of his or her own productive achievement. Beyond this liberal economic theory held that the rational balance of the entire economy as a whole, the adjustment of consumption and production, of supply and demand, resulted from the sum of individual rational economic decisions, so as to approximate, as if by the operation of an invisible hand, to a balance of full employment and an economic equilibrium between different regions. According to liberal theory the State could trust the recuperative powers of the market economy and limit itself to protecting the individual's freedom of initiative, above all the freedom of contract and the right to private property, and to respect everyone's equal rights before the law.

Catholic social teaching quickly became suspicious of this liberal model of society. It was only too obvious that the competition of the market economy did not neutralise but rather intensified the advantages that arose not so much from people's own achievement but much more from their family or connections, and that indeed it included a self-defeating tendency that transformed the initial advantages that arose from time to time into class privileges and thus favoured the personal and regional concentration of income, of the means of production and of economic power. Nor could it be disputed that workers' chances of finding a job or hanging on to the one they had got depended less on their personal readiness to exert themselves than on the social conditions of their surroundings, or that young people's chances of finding vocational training depended less on their own efforts than on whether they were boys or girls, where they were born, what their education was, and the occupation and income of their parents. It thus turned out that the individual rights of freedom applied both to those who had a permanent official post and their own home, who had been educated up to university level or were born in the city, and to those who had already been given notice, who lived in rented accommodation, who began their working life without employment or who grew up in border areas. The realisation thus grew that the proclamation of formal rights of freedom did not do anything to guarantee the real pre-conditions of freedom and legal security that the individual needs for the development of his or her personality and that the separation of the State and economic society that was a consistent consequence of the underlying liberal view had been overtaken by historical developments and had been transformed into a complicated relationship of mutual dependency.

Leo XIII had made clear the inadequacy of a formal guarantee of rights of freedom as well as the necessity of social action to correct the inequalities of wage-bargaining. If the labour contract depended on the agreement of partners in an unequal economic situation, then the agreement reached between employer and employee within the context of the State's guarantee of freedom of contract did not yet guarantee that the contract was just and equitable.[19] John XXIII looked for a harmonious reconciliation of the two aspects of State intervention, protecting the rights of the human person while also encouraging their exercise and at the same time preventing the danger of the rights of freedom being made use of without restraint: 'The exigencies of the common good further demand that a delicate balance be preserved by civil authorities in their efforts to co-ordinate and protect, and indeed to promote, the rights of citizens. An excessive concern for the rights of any particular individuals or sections of the community might well result in the principal amenities of the State being in effect monopolised by these citizens. Or again, the absurd situation can arise where the civil authorities, while taking measures to protect the rights of citizens, themselves stand in the way of the full exercise of these rights.'[20]

The tendency for European constitutions to try to balance these two poles is to be ascribed to the increased awareness of the growing gulf between constitutional theory on the liberal model and the social reality of industrial society, an awareness in which the

Church's proclamation of the social gospel has not been without influence. Thus the inclusion of the social welfare clause in the constitution of the German Federal Republic has the aim of allowing the State to intervene in free social transactions and obliging it to correct social inequalities that persist or arise in the maintenance of rights of freedom, as well as of guaranteeing the exercise of individual freedom for everyone. This does not mean discarding the bourgeois liberal idea of the constitutional State but (*Rechtsstaat*) but rather incorporating it in the new idea of the social welfare State. Just as the constitutional State was a product of the bourgeois revolution, so the social welfare State (*Sozialstaat*) is a product of industrial revolution. Just as the bourgeois constitutional State expressed the awareness of justice of the people of that time over against monarchical absolutism and compared with the latter represented a step forward, even if not the final stage of democracy, so the social welfare State, which secures the conditions that enable the individual to exercise his or her individual freedom, is a creative further development. Just as the constitutional State was concerned to exclude State intervention in the process of individual and social autonomy, so the social welfare State justifies the intervention of the State to protect and develop the freedom of the individual.[21]

(*c*) The conflict between labour and capital

The statements of the Church's teaching authority seems to blink a little when it is a question of distinguishing between rights of the worker and of the dependent employee, human rights derived from work and workers' rights derived from the relationship of wage labour. In the event the uncertainty is eliminated. For one thing the right to work is always mentioned in the context of a description of industrial society or of an appeal to the social welfare State to fulfil its obligations. Further, the concept of the indirect employer and the reference to the intricate complexity of the social organisation of work today show that it is the fundamental social right to work that is being talked about.

The proclamation of a fundamental social right to work corresponds to the resistance in solidarity to the one-sided distribution of opportunity at the start of the process of industrialisation during the last century. This one-sided distribution arose through the conflict between the small group of owners of capital who had the means of production at their disposal and the mass of industrial workers who were separated from the means of production and were forced to sell their labour.[22] In this situation the individual worker found himself in a double state of dependency with regard to the employer: his relationship to the demand for his labour and the income from it that served to maintain him was quite different from that of the employer to the demand for his goods, since the employer could if necessary sell up the means of production. Alongside this economic dependence was a technological dependence: with the conclusion of the labour contract the individual worker did not agree to specific detailed tasks but placed his labour totally at the disposal of the employer and at the same time submitted himself to being bossed around by the owners of the means of production.

For working people as a whole this dependency represented a class thing, the structural disadvantaging of dependent employees in a capitalist market economy. For a start the capitalist enterprise was organised exclusively from the capital side. The owner of capital claimed the exclusive right of decision about the volume and direction of production and thus about the level of employment and job structure. In keeping with this the income gained by production was divided between the capitalist's profit and the worker's wages; the regulation of production corresponding to the fluctuations of demand come after the making of profit. Furthermore, shares in the results of production were determined according to the way the income would be used. The wages that accrued to employees were predominantly made available for consumption while the profits that accrued to the employer were predominantly used for saving and investment. Finally the liberal State, by guaranteeing everyone the same rights of freedom, in fact favoured the owner of capital, who was thereby given a free hand to maximise profits and minimise wage costs, in other words to exploit his workers.

The decision of industrial workers not to overthrow capitalism by means of revolution but to reshape it by means of joint solidarity, building up power to counterbalance it, providing social correctives and the assumption of responsibility forms the starting point for a movement that has lasted for over a hundred years against the overweening power of the entrepreneur and the State. To begin with it was individual artisans who spontaneously laid down their work in order to improve their conditions of work and of life. Then despite the legal ban on combinations and strikes they came together to form regional associations, forged links between the regions and became permanently established. After the end of the First World War associations of workers were given constitutional recognition in Germany. Thereafter the democratic State emerged more and more from its neutrality and built up social welfare legislation. Finally workers were given rights of co-determination on the shop-floor, in the plant and in the company.

In this the organised labour movement has not contented itself with merely proclaiming the fundamental social right to work. By means of a complex strategy of regulating conflict it has itself undertaken its implementation.

4. CONSEQUENCES

Joint solidarity, building up a counterbalancing power in the context of free wage bargaining, social welfare policies on the part of the State and the introduction of co-determination have substantially improved the situation of the workers. But they have not removed the structural disadvantage at which they are placed in a capitalist market economy. Hence further practical and theoretical steps are desirable to bring about the implementation of the fundamental social right to work.

(a) The priority of employment policy

If work turns out to be the fulcrum and pivot of the entire social question, if it is approached in the perspective of the human person,[23] and if beyond this the rights of the worker over against the indirect employer are the fulcrum and pivot of social ethics,[24] then an active policy of full employment takes the first place in the list of economic political aims,[25] even if an effective policy of full employment is tied in with measures of financial policy, policy with regard to competition, structural policy with regard to different sectors and regions, as well as training policy. The institutions classified as indirect employers should draw up a comprehensive plan for the rational use of human labour in business undertakings. This would not subject all the competent authorities to public control but would rather distribute and co-ordinate them and guarantee the free initiatives of individuals, of dependent groups, and of local businesses and undertakings.[26] Beyond this international agreements are urgently needed on the new world economic order, which should not come about by the *diktat* of the industrialised countries but should rest on the balancing of interests in partnership between the industrialised and the developing countries.

(b) Legal formulation

Although the proclamation of a fundamental social right to work is not disputed by the Church's proclamation of the social gospel, the simultaneous mention of the State's policy of full employment or the linguistic reference to the indirect employer should indicate that, among the various possible ways of giving legal shape to a fundamental social right in constitutional terms, preference is given to the objective legal norm,

A *guarantee of establishment* that places the institutions concerned with unemployment insurance or labour exchanges under the special protection of the constitution and guarantees their essential existence is not excluded by the preferences and considerations of Catholic social teaching. A *subjectively public law* that gives the worker who is capable of working and wants to work a legally enforceable claim to the creation of a job opportunity is in practice undermined by the way in which such a claim is relative and depends on the economic situation[27] and by the indirect partner to the claim which can embrace a number of non-State bodies alongside the State itself.[28]

In view of these complementary considerations and limitations what presents itself as the suitable legal shape for a fundamental social right to work is the *objective legal norm* anchored in the constitution. Objective legal norms express duties on the part of the State that constitute directly valid constitutional law and become law capable of immediate implementation by means of detailed laws aimed at their reconciliation. Protection from unemployment, the idea of creating a job for every worker who is capable of working and willing to work, is stated to be a priority among the State's aims. Admittedly all that this directly involves is the subsequent legislation and the business of declaring unconstitutional legal decisions that run counter to it, but beyond this there are effects on the social partners that benefit the workers affected, even if they are not enforceable at law.

Translated by Robert Nowell

Notes

1. See *Kirchen kämpfen mit: die VWF-Focker-Aktion zur Erhaltung der Arbeitsplätze* ed. H. and H.-G. Ludwig (Mainz 1981); *Arbeitslosigkeit-ein Grund zum Protest; Dokumentation der Gronau-Aktion des Gesamtverbandes der katholischen Arbeitnehmer im Bistum Münster*, edited by the Kettelerhaus of the West German Catholic Workers' Movement (KAB) (Cologne 1982).
2. See H. Knapp *Grenzen kirchlicher Stellungnahmen* (Frankfurt-am-Main 1981).
3 Leo XIII *Rerum novarum* § 34.
4. Pius XII, Whitsun message 1941; see also John XXIII *Pacem in terris* §§ 18-20.
5. *Gaudium et spes* § 26.
6. *Ibid.* § 67.
7. John Paul II *Laborem exercens* § 16.
8. Pius XI *Quadragesimo anno* § 74.
9. See Pius XII, Whitsun message 1941.
10. John XXIII *Pacem in terris* § 64.
11. *Gaudium et spes* § 67.
12. John Paul II *Laborem exercens* § 18.
13. *Ibid.* § 17.
14. *Ibid.* § 18.
15. *Ibid.* § 18.
16. *Ibid.* § 9.
17. *Ibid.* § 6.
18. Paul VI *Populorum progressio* § 27.
19. See Leo XIII *Rerum novarum* § 34. Paul VI applied the same basic ideas to the contractual relationships at the world economic level between the industrialised and developing countries: Paul VI *Populorum progressio* §59.

20. John XXIII *Pacem in terris* § 65. Paul VI similarly accepts the possibility that the equality of citizens before the law serves as a pretext for discrimination and exploitation: 'Without a renewed education in solidarity, an over-emphasis of equality can give rise to an individualism in which each one claims his own rights without wishing to be answerable for the common good' (*Octogesima adveniens* § 23).

21. See M. Rath *Die Garantie des Rechts auf Arbeit* (Göttingen 1974); E. R. Huber 'Rechtsstaat und Sozialstaat in der modernen Industriegesellschaft' in *Rechtsstaatlichkeit und Sozialstaatlichkeit* ed. E. Forsthoff (Darmstadt 1968).

22. See John Paul II *Laborem exercens* §§ 8 and 11.

23. *Ibid.* § 3.

24. *Ibid.* § 17.

25. See Pius XII, Whitsun message 1941; John XXIII *Pacem in terris* § 64; *Gaudium et spes* § 67.

26. See John Paul II *Laborem exercens* § 18.

27. See *Gaudium et spes* § 67.

28. See Paul II *Laborem exercens* § 18; Pius XII, Whitsun message 1941.

C. Towards a New Theology of Work

Iring Fetscher

Changes in the Economic Meaning and Perceived Significance of Work

1. CHANGES IN THE CONDITIONS OF WORK IN THE LAST 200 YEARS

(a) Mechanisation and its Consequences

In the last 200 years there has been a change—fundamental and accelerating—in the *nature of work* which is necessary to supply the needs of human life. First the natural forces of wind and water were exploited for production. The ancient world was acquainted with water-mills, saluting them as liberating man from hard physical labour. Windmills were developed in the middle ages. Until the eighteenth century, however, most work was linked to the application of man's physical strength. The mechanical loom, preceded by the spinning machine, was the first to emancipate man's physical powers in the area of textile production. By breaking down work-processes into smaller and smaller partial tasks and recombining them in so-called 'manufactories' the way was being prepared for the introduction of more and more machines. The most important achievement of the eighteenth century was the *steam engine*, providing power for numerous mechanical processes. Following its exploitation to drive pumping, weaving and spinning machines, it was soon applied to transport, rendering the movement of goods easier, quicker and more regular. In the nineteenth century railways and steamship lines conquered whole continents and linked them together. Not until towards the end of the nineteenth century was electricity added as an important new source of power.

By mechanising labour, by dividing it into operations and subsequently recombining partial products—from the 'manufactories', via the early factories, the conveyor belt, up to the automated factory—production depended less and less on qualified craftsmanship and ultimately less and less on labour itself. First the application of *physical strength* became more and more superfluous, then the individual *skill*, the ability to carry out precise operations, was undermined by the unequalled precision of the machine. Finally in this century, and particularly in the last decades, even intelligence and neurophysical concentration has been replaced by electronic equipment. In the end, in many places of work, all that remains for the human worker to do is to keep an eye on the signals recording the production cycle and to deal with repairs.

As a result of these technological changes the *productivity* of human labour has been immensely increased. This has *shortened* the working time but above all it has created a huge increase in the availability of goods (and services), which has led, in many cases, to an over-saturated market in the consumer societies of highly industrialised countries. In order to dispose of the increased volume of goods the economy had continually to *cultivate new needs*. This was the purpose, for instance, of rapidly changing *fashions*. It was no accident that fashion was first brought to bear in the area of clothes, which was the first to be industrialised. Rapid changes of fashion then extend to other articles in so far as they could be produced industrially. The advertisements which increasingly urge us to 'change', to buy something 'new', would have seemed very strange to our grandparents as they furnished their homes. Earlier 'styles' encompassed whole centuries; today, even in furniture, styles change by decades. Vehicles (the quality of which, technically, has improved little in the last forty years) change their design with far greater frequency.

(*b*) Alienation from the Products of Work and Compensation through Consumption

A further cause of a growth in demand, while labour remains constant and productivity increases greatly, is that a large part of the population finds *no satisfaction* in its work. The *alienation* of workers from their product, from their work itself and from one another, first outlined by Marx, has grown greatly and embraces more and more of the population. We must not have a romantic view of the conditions of pre-industrial and pre-capitalist society, but we can surmise that direct satisfaction in the exercise of a craft was far greater than, e.g., that of a worker on a conveyor belt or of an office worker writing standard letters (or operating a word-processor). The *consumption* of countless products termed 'luxury' by the advertisements serves as compensation ('Go on—spoil yourself!') for this dissatisfaction and unease.

As the body, no longer taxed by physical work, needs the compensation of sport in order to remain healthy, so the dissatisfied spirit cries for luxuries. Here, for more and more people, work becomes a mere 'job', its only significance for the individual being in the *money* and the *possibilities of consumption*. Idealistic thinkers have interpreted technological advances as a means of overcoming the biblical curse 'In the sweat of your brow you shall eat your bread'. But in the middle-class view of work the disappearance of meaningful work is a *loss* to the individual. Even in industrialised society many are still primarily oriented to their own *achievement*. This is why members of the older generation like to describe society as a 'meritocracy'. This term implies that there is a recognisable causal connection between individual effort and achievement and material success such as social recognition. For many, however, this connection is no longer evident. Quite apart from the fact that the individual's possibilities of consumption scarcely correspond to the extent of his input, fewer and fewer younger people can accept work as providing a meaning for life. In part this may be connected with the fact that the meaning of existence presented by advertising (which dominates our society) is not work, but *consumption*. Partly, too, the consumer *avant-garde* presented in the glossy magazines are as a rule people of private means: people who live off the interest of their capital. The only people whose achievements give them a popular aura are pop-singers, film stars, top sportsmen and the like, i.e., generally those in the world of entertainment. Even the 'little man' can identify with them to the extent that he feels he can understand and imitate, in part, what they do. (This is especially applicable to football players, and the rock singers who are looked up to by many youngsters who also sing and play the guitar.)

(*c*) The Loss of Meaning in Work

Through the change in the shape of work and the rapid obsolescence of occupational patterns most people nowadays can no longer be sure of practising a trade once learned to the end of their working life. Even less frequently do we find a trade being handed down from parent to child. This was bound to diminish the younger generation's respect for the older, since the value of 'experience' had dwindled, not only in idea but in fact. One result is a widespread feeling of insecurity and disorientation. If all father and mother ever knew was a succession of mere 'jobs', they cannot provide a positive parental example to mould their children.

In the end what we have is a society which still requires of its members work in various forms, but can offer fully satisfying work only to a minority, holding on to the rest by means of consumer-style promises. Furthermore the system of wages and salaries is such that the few occupations which already bring satisfaction—leadership of all kinds, scientific and artistic work, etc.—are generally also those with the highest material rewards, whereas work, involving the *least satisfaction* is poorly paid as well. In explanation it is said, in economic terms, that scientific and artistic ability, like that of directing large businesses or institutions, is 'rare', or that the higher level of effort demanded in these areas can only be elicited by correspondingly higher material stimulants. Simple work requiring no qualifications, however, can be done by anyone and is cheaper because of the flooded labour pool. Consequently modern developed industrial society is divided in two in a further way, not envisaged by Marx, namely, into the small minority of those who find satisfaction in their work and thus can adhere to the middle-class conviction that the *meaning of life consists in productive achievement*, and the large majority who cannot echo these sentiments and yet are exhorted, nonetheless, to regard a person's work as what gives him value and respect. This lack of satisfaction because of the nature of work (its end-product is remote from the individual worker; it is obscure to him and seems part of the alien economic conditions which subjugate him) is intensified by the fact that a considerable number of people become unemployed during the recurrent cyclic and structural crises.

2. THE PROBLEM OF UNEMPLOYMENT

(*a*) The Economic Causes

It is true that in the welfare State every worker who becomes unemployed through economic conditions (or through accident or illness) has a right to a guaranteed maintenance without the stigma of accepting 'charity'. All the same the individual's social recognition still depends on his work—less on quality than on quantity. So, however far we have come from the 'Manchester' approach [regrettably, perhaps, Manchester has entered, through Marx into the German vocabulary as a symbol of exploitation—'*Manchestertum*' (translator)] with its cynical lack of concern for the unemployed and premature invalids, etc., to the present welfare State, the problem of unemployment remains unsolved. Finding work for the unemployed in State-sponsored projects, unless they can be seen to be both meaningful and necessary, is no solution. And at the same time the inner logic of the economic system presses more and more for machines and electronic devices, etc., to take over from the work force. Since wages and salaries are big cost factors in production, and since there is still intensive competition at least *between* the industrialised States, large corporations and businesses everywhere are anxious to replace workpeople (the euphemism is to 'free' them) through labour-saving processes. As a rule the work force needed to co-operate with the new labour-saving devices is far smaller than that replaced by them. Up to now this vicious circle has always been broken by an increased demand for, and a higher production of, consumer goods, i.e., the continual growth in volume of goods guaranteed the system's continued viability *and* some approximation to full employment. This solution, which has become more problematical in most countries in the last 20 to 30 years through State-financed defence spending (the 'consumer' aspect of which is a largely imaginary feeling of security) will be less and less possible in the future. In the face of the stress limits of the eco-sphere and the social limits of growth, to which Fred Hirsch has referred in his *Social Limits to Growth* (Cambridge, USA 1976), it is more and more urgently necessary to abandon the concept of a continual quantitative growth in production. To do so would by no means exclude development of production in the Third World; indirectly, it would benefit it. The Third World in no way needs labour-saving machines but rather, above all, so-called 'intermediate technology' which enables the masses of under-employed people to increase production of primary goods of all kinds. By contrast, to continue to increase production of more and more new luxury items for the populations of industrial States (items which necessarily lose their value the more common they are—since their value is exclusively one of prestige) is of no help to the distressed and starving populations of non-industrialised countries.

(*b*) The Requisite Corrections

Faced with 'quantitative growth limits' in the foreseeable future, what we need is a threefold corrective: in the distribution of work, in the quality of work, and in the evaluation of human activity ('praxis in the widest sense).

(i) As far as we can see, we can only cope with the continually slackening demand for workers—if we are to avoid huge permanent unemployment—by distributing this demand *equally* over the employable population, either by reducing the working week further (to 35 hours or even less) or by shortening the working life-span. Problems likely to arise here are discussed in (iii) below.

(ii) Much more important than the distribution of work to be done, is a *re-orientation* of scientific and technological development to create jobs providing a *satisfying, meaningful activity*. This would also result in a fall in the demand for compensatory consumer commodities; progress (just as desirable as ever) would be steered away from conflict with 'growth limits'.

(iii) Thirdly we need to take a further step towards the *re-orientation of values*. This requires us deliberately to turn away from the modern middle-class evaluation of man according to the material work he does, his 'product'; human 'praxis' is wider than material work. Certainly, man exhibits a practical intelligence which is *characteristic of him*; it marks him off from the animal world. But this distinctive activity must not be restricted—as happens widely in middle-class and in crude Marxist thought—to material work, work in the sense of satisfying material needs. In a deliberate rejection of the Soviet-Marxist narrowing of the view of man, Yugoslav philosophers like Gajo Petrović and Mihailo Marković have defined man as a 'practical being' in order to characterise the manifold richness of human existence. The restriction to material production—work—was typical of the early middle class in its endeavour to lift itself above the noble and 'spiritual' classes which were absolved from work. Crude Marxism does the same thing, by elevating the working class as the producer of all material goods to be the legitimate arbiter of society, while seeking to abolish a degenerate and parasitic middle class. Both of these inadequate views of human creativity and productivity are historically understandable; both have had equally dire consequences. It is essential to break free from them, as concrete examples will show: people rightly complain that our society has a low estimation of the work of a mother and housewife. As a result, feminists have demanded a 'housewife's salary', thus subscribing to the (conformist) view that social recognition is only achieved by activities which are *paid for*, i.e., salaried work. Humanistically speaking, what is perverse is not the demand itself but the prevailing mode of thought to which it clings. Must something be paid for in order to be valuable? Must all forms of human care, concern, goodness and kindness be converted into paid services before they can be recognised? Is it not rather a sign of increasing, cold inhumanity in human relations that people can offer themselves for money (through newspaper advertisements) simply to 'listen to' clients? That some contemporary of ours, cast upon the depths of his own isolation, finds it necessary to 'buy' a mere passive audience for his suffering? Does this not turn such 'service' into prostitution? Does behaviour only acquire value by being saleable—or is it not debased by being sold? This is not to reject the demand for the 'housewife's salary', for which there are valid arguments in social justice. Yet we must question the narrow view of man it manifests, measuring the social value of undertakings in terms of financial reward.

3. THE PERCEIVED SIGNIFICANCE OF WORK: TRANSITION FROM A MATERIAL TO A SOCIAL CULTURE

The narrowness can be overcome, however, by seeking the *authentic satisfaction* of human existence no longer in consumerism but in activity itself. Then recognition will no longer depend on income scale; personal behaviour, personal 'being' will be valued more than extrinsic 'having'. This is not to recommend a total rejection of the material aspect. Naturally, satisfaction of material needs is one of the preconditions of human existence. It is a necessary condition: it must not be made the sole content of existence. Besides material culture there is a social culture which blossoms upon it: but it can only do this if the former renounces all monopolistic aspirations. If an all-round shortening of working hours or working life-span were introduced, each individual would be given more and more scope to develop and exercise his human potential. He could spend time productively and creatively in science, the arts, social concerns, contemplation and interpretation—all modes of praxis—without thinking of acquiring income thereby. This is the only way to avoid the danger, implicit in extending the 'non-working' time, of creating a deliberate vacuum, made bearable only by the distraction of consumerism or some other anaesthetic. The disenchantment of portions of the younger generation with the 'meritocracy' may express—albeit at an instinctive and confused level—a dawning awareness of the necessity of a change of this kind.

The beginning of the middle class era saw the 'secular spirituality' of conscientious work, its success interpreted by Calvinists and Puritans as evidence of divine favour. History has put a question-mark behind this extreme view of the meaning of existence. Only a very small percentage of the population can affirm it in practice, and it imposes a psychic burden, furthermore, on the great majority of low wage-earners and above all on the unemployed. Having lost an inner relationship to meaningful work in which pride was taken, people turned away from the world of production and sought satisfaction in that of consumption, where ever-renewed promises of happiness are confronted with ever-recurring frustration and disappointment. Of its very nature the truly endless multiplication of consumer possibilities can never bring satisfaction and contentment. To overcome the dilemma of the affluent society we need to break out of the restricted view of man as *homo laborans*. The human being is defined by his human activity (praxis) but the latter must not be reduced to material work (i.e., the satisfaction of material needs). Such a restriction implies that only those activities (and 'services') which are paid for are recognised as valuable. Value here corresponds to the degree of remuneration. Clearly, a value-system of this kind conflicts with the morality we officially profess. But this dominant value-system according to income level and its consequent opportunities can only be overcome by a change in the socio-economic conditions which promote it. That is the clear necessity before us at the close of the middle-class era.

Translated by Graham Harrison

Dietmar Mieth

Solidarity and the Right to Work

HUMAN SOLIDARITY is one of the basic principles of Christian social ethics. This involves a double recognition: that people belong together on the basis of equal worth and that people must stand together in order to overcome their problems. But this concept of solidarity is still very general.[1] The solidarity of people will remain abstract unless it is applied to situations in which men rule over men and in which men only use other men for their own purposes. Solidarity is therefore not a diagnosis, but a concept of a goal. The collaboration of men in overcoming their problems can be recognised more strongly as the concept of a goal, which, in view of the conflicts between men, must appear abstract. Solidarity as abstract concept of a goal always runs the risk of hastily overleaping the concrete reality of defective solidarity.

Therefore it is necessary to make a distinction between *solidarity as first step towards an improvement in human conditions and solidarity as general goal*. In the first case the initial premiss is made of a defective reality, in the second that of an idea of a fulfilled life among men. The orientation to defective reality and the idea of a fulfilled reality may condition one another, but without doubt it is necessary to give precedence to concrete solidarity in conflicts over an abstract concept of a goal. For this reason *solidarity begins with the disadvantaged and hopes in this way to make a step towards a universal solidarity*.[2]

The precedence of the claim of the disadvantaged to solidarity[3] has the effect, in the dimension of work and unemployment, that the needs of those people take precedence who are most disadvantaged by the international labour market situation. The principle of solidarity therefore supports the maxim of justice, of seeking the greatest good for the most disadvantaged.[4] This ethical maxim coincides in its turn with the maxim of a liberation theology which is described generally as 'option for the poor'. This theological-ethical maxim presupposes, of course, that the first step in the practical conversion in this direction has already been accomplished. Solidarity in the Christian context is not merely a maxim of conviction, but the result of a new praxis which is already at work. Such solidarity is not an imposed moral duty, but the unavoidable answer to the claims of the Christian faith, on the basis of which what is actually humanly self-evident is not only recognisable, but practicable.

If solidarity is linked with the right to work, then essentially two questions arise: we should ask how, through an employment policy of solidarity the right to work can best be carried out; but we must also ask what conflicts human solidarity can find itself in with the right to work. For an understanding of the right to work at the expense of others would be a violation of the maxim of solidarity. Therefore it is important for us first of all to examine solidarity in conflict.

1. SOLIDARITY IN CONFLICT

It is doubtless right for workers to support the maintenance or expansion of employment in solidarity with one another. Doubtless it is just as right that the unemployed, in solidarity with one another, strive together for conditions in which they can find decent work and hence for themselves and their families a real right to live and a human identity. It is, however, conceivable that the *achievement of the right of one can lead to a decrease in the right of another*. There have been some such cases in the national and in the international sphere. The question is, which priorities should be applied here.

Among the cases in which solidarity is difficult belong the increasing unemployment, in particular of young people, women and older workers.[5] Thus, for example, competition in the financing of jobs and training positions can occur, in particular if State subsidies and measures for the maintenance or promotion of training positions are not adequate. For the sake of insertion into the working world it can be necessary for young people to take on short-contract work. The creation of jobs for young people can possibly lead to considering the premature phasing-out of older people from their jobs. But it is precisely here that the question arises of whether this premature phasing-out might not be connected with severe existential difficulties for the older workers concerned. Women's right to work raises further problems: at the international level it is still in places much too little recognised and enforced; it can, if it refers only to non-domestic work, lead to a narrowing of the view of woman's service in the family. This is quite largely due to the fact that the right to work is very strongly modelled on the role of the man, which in its turn makes it difficult for a man to contemplate renouncing professional advancement in favour of his wife. Nevertheless, the right of women to work must be taken particularly seriously as an independent right. Where there is high unemployment the danger often exists that the right to work is granted only to one person in the family or to single people. This very quickly leads to a closing of ranks of workers' solidarity, to the exclusion of the married woman's job. It is well known that solidarity with the right to work of others becomes problematical in any country where the right to work of foreigners is concerned.[6] Foreigners are frequently used as pawns in employment policy. Employment policies involving restrictions are carried out on the backs of foreigners. It is certainly not easy to set priorities here under the maxim of solidarity, but in any case someone who has entered the job world, with all duties and rights, who by his efforts has earned the same claims as other national workers, should no longer be disadvantaged in his rights.[7] As soon as solidarity of working people is merged with national solidarity, the conflict is shifted to a false level, for national solidarity should not be in opposition to human rights[8]—on the contrary, it exists in order that people can live together in justice.

The relationship of solidarity and the right to work becomes particularly problematic if it is applied to *international relations*. A striking example of this is in the securing of jobs in the field of manufacture of so-called 'defence engineering' products. In the industrialised countries huge amounts of armaments are manufactured and exported. Even though this branch of the economy, in relation to the overall economy, is only of relatively minor importance, it can nevertheless easily be regarded, on the basis of its growth rate, as a place where job security and expansion are possible in a special way. But precisely here the evil results are obvious. Human solidarity with the disadvantaged in the Third World, where most of these exported weapons are used, is in conflict with the solidarity of the people working in this branch of the economy with one another.

Here the question arises of whether solidarity can be divided. It is certainly not divisible if the right to live of people is definitely affected. But it is possible for union movements who place particular value on their international solidarity with working people to be blind to the effect in the international field of a strict execution of the right to work at local level. This dilemma is particularly acute if too little restriction is placed, for political and economic reasons, on arms exports from industrialised countries.

Less obvious, but basically almost just as problematic, is the whole question of *the securing of jobs by the export economy*. As long as the export economy is balanced out within common markets using the maxim of reciprocity, the possibility exists of political control of economic expansion. But it is precisely exports from the industrialised countries to Third World countries which involve an increase in debts, leading their national economy into an ever more difficult situation. Economic dependence has a decisive effect on the labour market situation of the countries of the Third World. Here again it is certainly very difficult to uphold the maxim of solidarity towards the disadvantaged in the consciousness of the working people of the industrialised countries. And conversely, the creation of jobs by multinational firms in Third World countries can work out just as ambivalently.[9] The shift of promotion to regions in which lower wages can be paid means again a reduction in jobs in the industrialised countries. This, too, is a phenomenon which makes the solidarity of working people with the disadvantaged or jobless particularly difficult.

Therefore it is clear that not the least reason why solidarity of working people in relation to the right to work is so difficult is because for people in a situation of job competition charity begins at home, i.e., because in general they want to enforce their own right to work at the expense of others. *The conflicts of solidarity are primarily structural conflicts*. Structural conflicts can, however, only be overcome by more equitable economic relations and by an international alignment of employment policies. Nevertheless, the solidarity of working people can also ease the solution of problems in certain areas. This applies, for example, for solving problems such as job sharing or the shortening of the working week.[10] It is scarcely possible for solidarity with the right to work to be achieved without the readiness to place restrictions on oneself. This holds both in the national and in the international field.

2. OBSTRUCTION OF SOLIDARITY

Solidarity in the right to work seems today to be obstructed essentially by three factors. The first factor is an entrepreneurial structure which makes a sharp distinction between *responsibility for its own economic sphere and responsibility for the sphere of job structuring*. This separates the solidarity of working people from the effects of the economic factors on the position of working people. The path to solidarity in the right to work must therefore lead via some involvement in national policies. But for most working people this is only a very indirect involvement. For the individual working person little possibility exists of achieving clarity with regard to the problem of the relations of one's own work to the right to work of others, especially if this problem extends into the international sphere. The division of solidarity and economic efficiency, which finds its basis in the confrontation of the social partners, can only be removed if the *claim of the priority of work over other productive forces*, which for some time now has been raised more and more clearly on the part of Catholic social theory, can finally be honoured.[11] Solidarity in the right to work presupposes the priority of the economic factor of work over other economic factors. Otherwise not only does economic expansion have priority over employment policy, but it also appears as the primary means of solving the problems of this employment policy.[12] Furthermore, through the division of economic and social responsibility, the claims of the social partners on one another are in fact identified. More pay will, for example, become more important than the demand for the right to work.

A second factor is the lack of *balance of markets*. The monopolisation of products and prices by groups of undertakings involves a decrease in the total number of companies, especially of smaller and medium-size companies, which contribute most to a dispersion of jobs. The imbalance in the international market situation, especially between countries of the First and Third Worlds, has been attacked often enough. The policy of development aid has proved inadequate to solve this problem, as the promotion of the weak has entailed an expansion of the strong. For that reason both internal and external economic imbalances have been not decreased, but increased. However, a certain new orientation of development policy in the direction of promoting employment, a more equitable distribution of income and satisfaction of basic needs can be observed. These problems can, however, in the long run be solved not by single measures, but only by a strengthening of the international authorities and by a more equitable world economic order.

The *transfer of technology* can certainly be named as the third factor. The development of new technologies, especially in the field of information processing, certainly also belongs, in addition to the price increases of raw materials, to the structural conditions which also have their effect on the present striking growth in unemployment.[13] But whereas in the industrialised countries the development of new technologies also includes the development of new production plant, the developing countries are almost totally excluded from this partial redirection. The new technologies therefore become a decisive factor of a new expansion economy which will only increase market imbalances even more. The report of the International Labour Office on employment policy arrives therefore at the following opinion in regard to the problem of technology transfer: 'Until the developed countries show a more favourable attitude towards a new world economic order, which would create greater international justice, information technology and its applications will probably increase even more the economic inequalities between less developed and industrially advanced countries.'[14] Such an increasing inequality is, however, also an obstacle to solidarity with the right to work in these countries.

3. SOLIDARITY AS SELF-LIMITATION

In addition to the structural change in their economic conditions, solidarity in the right to work also demands *a readiness to limit and restrict oneself*. That solidarity demands sacrifices is a familiar truism, a favourite in all sorts of State and even ecclesiastical documents.[15] This appeal can of course easily be misunderstood as meaning that it is a matter of distributing the want among those already most affected by it. In the mutual implication of solidarity and self-limitation, however, more is at stake: it is a matter of discovering *the limits of a system* which hitherto inextricably bound the emancipation of the right to work with the law of economic growth. The demand for solidarity by self-limitation first of all bears on the forced growth of the economy. Here it is not a matter of an option of growth or contraction.[16] In economics there is no doubt that receding movements of the economy are just as dangerous as a heedless promotion of the forces of growth of the capitalist economy. It is, however, important to alter growth qualitatively in such a way that, for example, investments are planned so that they reduce not the use of labour, but the use of energy and raw materials. The aims of stabilising energy, of more equitable distribution of income and a securing or creation of jobs must be balanced out with one another. The greater the distribution of energy sources, the wider the supply of jobs can be. The smaller the dependence on the transfer of a few energies, the more favourable the position for economic self-sufficiency. That means a stronger regionalisation of the economy and of employment policies. If need be, partial regional autonomy must be assured by a more equitable world economic order, in which the distribution of labour is more important than the rapid expansion of the economy. All this is easier said than done, for it presupposes a definite change in consciousness of the populations in the industrialised countries. Here it is not so much a matter of the readiness of the individual to act more sparingly in his own sphere and to renounce some consumer goods, but more a matter of the capacity on the part of the majority to adopt a policy which is based on the view that today's effects of the expansion economy on the position of the population of the Third World can be tomorrow's effects for their own economy. Precisely where a certain threshold of utility of consumer goods has been reached, the view grows that an increase in consumption in the long run does not serve one's own interests, but is merely an expression of the urge for expansion of certain branches of the economy. If the real benefit of goods is determined not by their possession but by their use, then in the consumer society, too, a use of goods is conceivable which sees individual need secured in common possession. As farming associations can share larger equipment, without individuals losing anything, so it is also conceivable that households can better exploit larger items of equipment by having joint use of them. The securing of jobs by a high quantitative output of consumer goods could give way here to the priority of a higher degree of production quality and durability, through which jobs will be secured in a different way.

Solidarity and self-limitation, however, all concern the work of the individual person himself. Meritocracy, bound up as it is with the structures of superordination and subordination, as well as of competition, presupposes a working man who regards professional advancement as an actual identity bonus. More and more people, however, are coming to the view that advancement by tough competition does not represent the ultimate yardstick of quality and life. They see that work can not only bring an identity bonus, but also demolish one's own identity if it is advanced at the expense of human solidarity. Every gain in prestige at work is linked at the same time with a discrimination against others' work. Solidarity in work should reduce the barriers between working people and not strengthen them. The more the humanisation of jobs progresses, the less will it be necessary to stake one's whole existence on the fight for better jobs. While on the one hand self-realisation in work and at one's job must be improved, on the other hand the view should recede that self-realisation can only be secured on the basis of work. However much we advocate the right to work, *we also need a limitation of the expectations placed upon the realisation of that right.* The human being cannot understand himself on the basis of his work alone. On the other hand, however, he should not place too many expectations in an increase in leisure time, which for its part is understood mainly as an industrial marketing area. *Solidarity as self-limitation demands a new understanding of the identity of man.* This identity should above all be understood as solidary identity.[17] It is not work that makes life sweet but the interaction and communication possible in work. The same holds for leisure-time relations, in which the relations of the working world are reflected. Solidarity as self-restriction would therefore presuppose a change in the structure and rhythm of work. There are various models for the humanisation of work which contain the seeds of this. Thus, for example: sovereignty over the distribution over one's own work-time, conscious collaboration on shared jobs, the partially autonomous work-group which produces a product jointly from beginning to end. Solidarity as self-limitation demands that *interaction and communication take precedence over output and prestige.*

4. CHRISTIAN SOLIDARITY AND THEOLOGY OF WORK

Christian solidarity realises the high ethos of charity.[18] It cannot rest at recognising the right of others, but also encourages others to be accepted as human beings by other human beings. Such a solidarity is faced today with a dilemma: on the one hand it should be carried out concretely, i.e., face to face, therefore be solidarity of people working together. On the other hand it demands, especially in the industrialised countries of the First World, solidarity with the 'farthest', i.e., with the disadvantaged on the periphery of the world economic system. We have seen that both can come into conflict with one another. This dilemma can only be overcome through a step by step expansion of the limits of the current solidarity. The more working people extend their solidarity to the unemployed in their community and in their region, the more they will recognise that *any solidarity must be a solidarity for others.* Christian solidarity proves the inner power of its cohesion in its external effects, for it is here that we find a progressive removal of the obvious indifferences of our life. There are no possessions for which someone else must not help to carry the cost. 'Idols,' says a pastoral letter of the Dutch bishops, 'can be recognised by the fact that in the long run they destroy solidarity among people.'[19] Such an idol is the protection of possessions at the expense of others. True solidarity presupposes that the other is aware that he is also included in what we demand. Therefore we can demand our own right to work all the more that this guarantees the possibility of the right to work of others.

If this is presupposed, *a theology of work may no longer be developed, as previously, in relation to the individual man*. If two theological presuppositions are right, i.e., that man as image of the active creator God must initially and primarily be understood as community and, secondly, in this community also represents the collaboration of a trinitarian God, then work can no longer simply be understood as act of the creative self-realisation of the individual in the realisation of the divine task of creation and in the preparation of the eschatological penetration of creation through reconciliation. That the human being was created from the beginning as man and woman with equal worth and that this creation from the outset contains self-transcendence towards others (see Gen. 1:26-28) also has a bearing on the theological understanding of work. *Work is not so much place of self-realisation as place of social self-achievement.*[20] It must be understood theologically as place of solidary identity-forming. Where work isolates it is not fulfilling the meaning of creation. Where work creates relations, where it allows the human being to become himself through other human beings, where work is more than human beings dealing with technical equipment, then it leads together what God has bound. This means for the right to work that it must be understood from the point of view of Christian solidarity as a right which proves to be just because it is being claimed for others. In the context of a Christian understanding of human solidarity and of a Christian theology of work we should therefore ask ourselves how far our work promotes the right to work of others and precisely in that is a sign that is part of the creative activity of God.

Translated by Della Couling

Notes

1. On the concept of solidarity, see K. E. Løgstrup 'Solidarität und Liebe' *Christlicher Glaube in moderner Gesellschaft* ed. F. Böckle *et al.* (Freiburg i. Br. 1982) xvi pp. 97-128. We are not starting from the sociological concept of solidarity, according to which the intensity of mutual

dependence, common interests and mutual obligation creates solidarity, but from an ethically unambiguous concept, which transcends the sociological ambiguity. See on the sociological concept M. Weber *Wirtschaft und Gesellschaft* (Tübingen 1976) p. 25.

2. Universality and solidarity seem to contradict one another, if solidarity is understood primarily as distinguishing feature between a social system and its environment (e.g., in T. Parsons *The Social System* (Glencoe 1951)). But if solidarity is applied to common human worth, as occurs in the tradition of Christian social theory (see *Laborem excercens* § 8), then it is always solidarity in an open movement from inner bond (commitment) and strength to universal community of interests. If the movement towards universality alone is attended to, the concept of solidarity loses its strengh; if the degree of intensity of the inner relation alone is attended to, the concept of solidarity loses its ethical dimension, as can be seen in the borderline case of the solidarity of criminals and terrorists (see K. E. Løgstrup, *op. cit.*, pp. 101-103).

3. Solidarity, since in modern times it has been understood as relation of the equal-placed and equal-minded, has always had an emancipatory character, i.e., it acts to remove limits on freedom.

4. J. Rawls *A Theory of Justice* (Harvard 1971).

5. See Report VI (1) of the International Labour Office, Geneva, for the Sixty-Ninth Session of the International Labour Conference of 1983 on employment policy (Geneva 1982) pp. 98-108. The report includes women, young people and older workers as 'vulnerable groups'; also migrant workers and the disabled. See also C. Offe *Opfer des Arbeitsmarktes, Zur Theorie der strukturierten Arbeitslosigkeit* (Neuwied, Darmstadt 1977).

6. Another problem is the racist restriction of the labour market. According to press reports, up to 60 per cent of coloured young people under twenty years of age in the big cities of the USA are unemployed.

7. On the profits obtained by countries from foreign workers, the report cited in note 5 states (p. 119): 'There can for example be no question that Switzerland, without the influx of over 8·5 million normal workers, seasonal workers or frontier-crossers, since the Second World War, would not enjoy the present level of prosperity and command the same infrastructure and industry of the present service sector. Nor could Saudi-Arabia achieve the goals set in its third five-year plan without the aid of at least a million foreigners in the period 1980-1985. Furthermore, the profit for the employing countries is owing not only to the institutional procedure which links up the absorption of foreign workers with production, but also to the fact that the expense is saved of training the labour force before its entry into the country; furthermore, the employing countries gain extraordinarily hard-working and undemanding workers.'

8. Which is why the recommendation of the ILO (International Labour Organisation) said of the employment policy of 9.7.1964, VI, 32 (1): 'The industrialised countries should in their economic policies, including their policies of economic collaboration and market promotion, take into account the necessity of promoting employment in other countries, in particular in developing countries.'

9. On the role of the multinationals, the pastoral letter of the Dutch bishops 'Human beings in the working world' (Lent 1980) notes: 'In recent times in particular the transnational undertakings have become so powerful in the social and political sphere that certain aspects of rights and freedoms are also in part governed by them.' This occurs to the good and to the bad, but in any case with precedence given to economic efficiency and with a lack of politico-ethical control.

10. See Chr Gremmels and Fr Seghers 'Arbeitslosigkeit—Herausforderung der Kirchen' *Gesellschaft und Theologie*, Abteilung Sozialethik, no. 11 (Munich/Mainz 1979) pp. 185-193, on 'strategies against unemployment'.

11. See John Paul II *Laborem excercens* (1981) § 12.

12. There are three reasons why unemployment in the Eighties can no longer be solved by economic expansion: a growth rate comparable to that of the Fifties can no longer be expected (and anyway it would only benefit the industrialised countries); growth in productivity and increase in the number of jobs are mutually incompatible and this is mainly because of rationalisation investments; economic growth, in view of the scarcity of resources, ecological results and increase

in the imbalances between the First and Third Worlds, has become questionable. (See Gremmels, Seghers, in the article cited in note 10, pp. 180 ff.)

13. See the report, cited in note 5, of the International Labour Office, pp. 39-53, on 'Choice, development and transfer of technology'. The counter-effect would have to be carried out by means of a labour-intensive employment policy. The report quotes models from China and Japan which consist mainly in promoting a technologically advanced, decentralised small industry.

14. The report cited in note 5, p. 48.

15. See the pastoral letter cited in note 9, pp. 47 ff.

16. See *Wege aus der Wohlstandsfalle, Der NAWU-Report: Strategien gegen Arbeitslosigkeit und Umweltzerstörung* eds. H. Chr. Binswanger *et al.* (Frankfurt a.M. 1979) pp. 110 ff.

17. See on the idea of solidary identity in particular: Pl. Spescha 'Arbeit-Freizeit-Sozialzeit Die Zeitstruktur des Alltags als Problem ethischer Verantwortung', *Europäische Hochschulschriften*, vol. 156 (Bern/Frankfurt a.M./Las Vegas 1981) pp. 155-230. Spescha presents the experience of solidary identity in terms of its socio-psychological sources and its theological disclosure as basic experience for the integration of work, freedom and communication.

18. See K. Løgstrup, *op. cit.*, p. 114. I do not agree with Løgstrup's presupposition that 'one's neighbour . . . can be anybody'. One's neighbour is rather, according to the parable of the Samaritan, someone who is unavoidably in my path and I may not make any distinction with him.

19. Cited in note 9, p. 34.

20. By social self-achievement I understand a forming of the self out of interaction and communication which nevertheless does not hinder but promote the consistency and continuity of the human subject. See D. Mieth *Epik und Ethik, Eine theologisch-ethische Interpretation der Josephromane Thomas Manns* (Tübingen 1976) pp. 148-188.

Giannino Piana

Human Work: Blessing and/or Curse?

WESTERN THOUGHT wavers continually between two opposite attitudes to work. There is the pessimistic vision of work based on a cosmological and anthropological dualism in the Platonic and Cartesian tradition and the exaltation of work as the place which characterises and defines the specificity of the human being.

The arrival of industrial society gave place at first to the development of a true mysticism of work fed in part by Christian thought itself. The transformation of profession (*Beruf*) into 'vocation' by the great reformers required the creation of a work ethic centred on the control of the use of time with the abolition of *otium*, hard work and the accumulation of goods, and even including saving up money and sobriety of life.[1]

There has been an exaggerated stress on work which finds its expression either in describing all human activity as 'work' or in making work the centre towards which all human life gravitates. This procedure is justified both by a Hegelian analysis which sees work as the expression of the human struggle against materiality to affirm our own free subjectivity, and above all, by a Marxian analysis which transfers the imputation of the alienating character of work onto the social organisation and thus transforms work into the privileged area in which the political objective of human liberation can be realised. However, the limits of such interpretations soon become apparent. The polemical voices which criticised *homo faber* and denounced the technical spirit since the beginning of our century have acquired a prophetic value. In industrial or post-industrial society work has in fact undergone a process of progressive deterioration. The repetitive nature of work caused by automation, the manipulation of the person arising from the technological apparatus, the development model which, instead of expanding the capacity for free personal options, increases forms of human objectivisation and produces growing contradictions, are all symptoms of a growing uneasiness. The changes which have taken place during these years both in the organisation of work and in technological development have brought about new forms of alienation and frustration, characterised by insecurity and psychological stress.[2]

Attitudes and behaviour towards work in the subjective sphere (absenteeism, allergies, negativity, etc.) show the deterioration of the value 'work' on the individual and social level and make us suspect that this value may now be irremediable and that we should move in the direction of a liberation *from* work instead of insisting on an impossible liberation *of* work. In other words there is a tendency now to reject work as the place to seek subjective personal identity and as the place in which to operate a project for political change. The ideological crisis of scientific and technological progress and the questioning of the neo-illuministic hypothesis underlying it—a hypothesis which succeeded in mortifying rationality by reducing it to instrumental reason—coincides with the superceding of a 'work culture' as a myth or value in itself. Thus the interpretation of the historical dialectic as a dialectic centred upon work is disputed and more attention is being paid to other dimensions of human experience, such as *eros*, play, celebration and free time, as alternative and authentically humanising activities.[3]

1. THE AMBIVALENCES OF THE CHRISTIAN TRADITION

In the tendency to polarise attention upon one or the other of the two aspects of work, as either a liberating force or an instrument of personal alienation, both poles appeal to Christian tradition. For a long time the Church cultivated a pessimistic view of work (under the influence of the dominant culture). It saw only the aspect of condemnation and curse for human sin and regarded work in a purely individualistic and spiritualistic light. This view totally lacked a vision of work as an objective and collective operation which produced a particular human environment and thus reproduced the mode of spiritual life, human culture and spiritual needs. This view also lacked a vision of work as taking place within a particular society, i.e., in a particular historical context. The ethics and spirituality deriving from this view of work concentrated exclusively on the subjective intentions of the worker and completely disregarded the significance of the product of his labour.

The 'theology of work' rightly reacted against this view. This theology was developed in the Fifties as a result of deeper and more systemative reflection on the positive nature of earthly realities and the necessity for Christians to be seriously involved with them.[4] In this context work acquires full human dignity in the sense that it comes to be regarded as the environment within which human beings become conscious of themselves and direct their own lives. Technological progress itself was exalted as an increase in knowledge, a means of discovering the truth, a 'discovery' made through the transformation of the energies of nature: the condition of *homo artifex* in his attempt to rationalise the *cosmos* and to set new processes of socialisation in motion becomes an epiphany of human powers.

This humanising task which belongs to work in its anthropologising definition finds a deeper legitimisation in the context of Christian revelation. God has called man to fulfil his saving, creative and redemptive plan by means of human work, in which we can realise ourselves as persons through the mastery over nature, and at the same time become socialised by our relationships with others and strive for the growth of justice and solidarity. Thus 'the work which the Christian saw in his catechism and in his religious behaviour exclusively as a burdensome task done "by the sweat of his brow", as a punishment through a mysterious collective infrastructure (see the homiletic literature of the nineteenth century) now becomes part of that creative activity in which man in his expansive power and his technical and economic creativity is God's partner or, in biblical language, God's image. We can also say that in this right view of the function and nature of work in the construction of the world, the theology of creation has regained its full truth. As against a spirituality which placed the Genesis story in a previous chapter and completely blocked the whole Christian mystery of the redemption, through this re-valuing of work, creation and incarnation are now seen as the two sides of a single undertaking, in which the reason for the incarnation and its purpose is a "new creation".'[5]

This theology was officially taken up by Vatican II, which set work in close connection with 'Christian newness', that is the believer's vocation to build a new world, in which interpersonal relations and man's relationship with nature will rediscover their original space and fullness of meaning.[6] Thus the foundations are laid for a definitive connection between the theme of work and the theme of history: a connection which post-conciliar theology did not fail to develop and in which it stressed the political-social problems rather than the problems of the relationship between man and nature.

2. IN SEARCH OF A NEW BALANCE

Now we are seeing the negative and worrying side of the latter problem, because of the introduction of complex and contradictory systems for the manipulation of nature. In recent years this has given rise to a less optimistic attitude to work. The need is seen to pay more attention to its ambiguities.

In fact these ambiguities are already clearly expressed in the message of revelation, in which work is both the prolongation of the work of creation and the place where man's alienated condition becomes most clearly visible. Terms used by the Bible to designate work are eloquent in this respect. 'In this elementary context, which nevertheless offers a large range of meaning,' observes Chénu, 'we may set and interpret the two words used for work in biblical terminology: *mēlā'kâ*, which is used in relation to the work of creation to express God's presence in history, the working out of his plan which began at the creation; and *sabōdâ* which indicates servitude, slavery, including the enslavement to Nebuchadnezzar. The interaction of these two terms, their mixing in a play of paradoxes, is the law which forms history, which is both free and determined, both independent justice and irreparable destiny. This is how the prophets view the double condition of work: it is a service in which man realises his dignity and moving sand in which he flounders. This double meaning of work is also found in Greek, where a distinction is made between labour (which is heavy and binding, χοπιάω) and *work* (which is fulfilling, brings happiness and is a way to perfection, ἐργάζομαι).'[7]

The Old Testament wavers continually between these two opposite views. Whereas the Priestly Tradition (Gen. 1) derives work from God's commandment and connects it with God's own working, thus recognising it as the instrument through which man develops God's image, the Jahvist Tradition (Gen. 2-3) stresses the burdensome nature of work, interpreting it as the consequence of a curse upon the earth caused by sin, which places mankind in a hostile relationship with the earth. The creation was willed by God for man who was called to exercise an activity (to tend and cultivate), which makes him God's collaborator in the progressive organisation of the universe. But sin has introduced an element of serious tension into human experience: a tension which runs through human relationships and the relationship between man and the cosmos. Work is now painful and often sterile, it is one of the areas over which sin now wields its greatest power. The pain is the price man must pay for the power God has given him over creation: the power remains but the cursed soil resists and must be conquered (Gen. 3:17).

The New Testament position is similar. The coming of Jesus projected onto work the paradoxes and illuminations of the Gospel. Work in the New Testament is both exalted and ignored, as if it were an unimportant detail. It is exalted through the example of Jesus, the workman (Mark 6:3) and son of a workman (Matt. 13:55) and through the example of Paul who works with his hands (Acts 18:3) and boasts about it (Acts 20:34; 1 Cor. 4:12). Nevertheless on the subject of work the Gospels maintain an impressive silence. They seem not to know the word except to designate the works to which we should apply ourselves and these are the works of God (John 5:17; 6:28) or to indicate as an example the birds of the air 'who neither sow nor reap' (Matt. 6:26) or the lilies of the field 'who toil not, neither do they spin' (Matt. 6:28).

These are not contradictions but two poles of a Christian attitude. The coming of the kingdom makes everything else that does not go in its direction relative. Work is not de-valued but put in its proper place. It still has its original significance but its full meaning is to be found in the mystery of Christ, that is in the context of the incarnation and redemption, thereby retaining its double character of human fulfilment and suffering.[8]

Thus in Christian thought work has positive and negative values. It is both the place where human growth can occur and the place where we feel most heavily the weight of sin, not only because work is burdensome and makes us suffer but especially because it contains the risk of alienation and the illusion of Prometheus. As G. Angelini rightly stresses, 'the particular activity which is work constitutes a particular moment in the pursuit of possible goods by human freedom and at the same time manifests one of the possible and most conspicuous forms of that Protean deception which is the sin of Adam. . . . By its nature work bears within it the radical possibility of 'alienation': work is not immediate enjoyment, a relationship with the world which immediately coincides with man's being-for-himself; work is an objective and instrumental action directed towards this enjoyment, which means that it is possible for others to take possession of my work or for me to do the work without thinking of it as my work, i.e., man can be estranged from his work. On the other hand, the number of goods that work can make accessible to man is indefinite or, in terms which are only apparently different—the struggle against the hindrances and uncertainties that occur in the effort to possess securely certain possible goods, does not have predefined limits. This space of 'indefiniteness' leads to the illusion that work actively can simply cancel the evil in man's life, or procure him salvation; work can insinuate the temptation: 'You will be like gods'.[9]

3. IN THE DYNAMISM OF THE MYSTERY OF THE TRINITY

These two attitudes to work which are present throughout Christian tradition and are amply confirmed in our present socio-cultural context, require for their correct understanding a more precise insertion of human work into the context of the Gospel. In other words we need to rethink human work in the light of a re-reading, from the salvation history point of view, of the mystery of God, which is the mystery of the Trinity. In fact human work acquires its full significance as work in the context of the divine *opus*, the work begun by the Father in the creation, completed by the Word, which took flesh in Jesus of Nazareth, and called to attain its fullness through the action of the Spirit, who acts in history through the building of the Kingdom. In the strong sense, Christianity is 'memory' and as such refers back to a past to be actualised in the present in a continual effort towards creative openness to the future. Human work is the space where creation, which found its most authentic face in Christ, is led by the Spirit to its definitive end: the consummation of all things in the Lord and in communion with him, the restoration of the perfect identity of man and the world.

Redefining work in the light of the mystery of the Trinity means recuperating its creational, redemptive and eschatological dimensions in a dialectical and fruitful relationship which does not exaggerate either pole but releases the dynamic tensions which add up to the whole of human experience.

The sometimes optimistic, sometimes pessimistic attitudes which we have seen in Christian tradition have their origin in the one-sided emphasis on either the creational or the redemptive aspect but they also pay insufficient attention to the eschatological aspect as a prolongation of the work of the Spirit: an aspect which gives work a new dimension by introducing side by side with material need the historical task of transforming the cosmos, the no less important need to wait for the future of God as the absolutely free gift, who will then abolish the tension between work and contemplation.

From this articulated vision of work in the complex context of the Christian mystery a few important ethical consequences derive and these ought to be mentioned, at least schematically.

(*a*) It seems necessary to stress the *relativity of work*, as a fundamental moment of human affirmation and liberation, which does not, however, exhaust man's totality, his possibilities of self-realisation. The interpretation of human life as a task does of course give high value to the activity of work. But this does not mean work is not also simultaneously a state of necessity and alienation. Furthermore—as F. Totaro acutely observes—'the ambiguity of work permeates the whole of Marxian thought. This explains the apparent contradiction in the two concepts of work elaborated by Marx. When he is thinking of the model of creative work, he gives it credit as a universal human activity or as a polyvalent activity in which the whole range of the practical possibilities of the individual may be expressed. When he is thinking of work as a material necessity, which will remain even in post-capitalistic society, he proposes its reduction to a minimum, especially with the help of the growth of technology. This will mean that material needs can be satisfied through the expense of an increasingly negligible amount of time and so free human activity can be expanded. Creative work and instrumental work remain in Marx as two irreducibles and this irreducibility has repercussions on the more or less Utopian curve which his writings on the problem of work assume.'[10]

(*b*) In this context we see clearly that the meaning of work must be sought through a constant *dialectic between work time and non-working time*, between liberation *of* work and liberation *from* work. Polarising the attention onto one side or the other causes serious ambiguity, because liberating ourselves from work looks much more like an allegory than an approximation but the liberation of work is also certainly an approximation. On the one hand we must recognise the irreplaceable value of work for human growth but we must also realise that the moment of rest, relaxation, worship is just as essential for our humanisation. In other words we must realise that work becomes true and authentic in a certain sense by negating itself, by means of a process which is both abolition and affirmation, in that by becoming rest, it becomes a time of culture and of worship, a time of the spirit and thus human time.

(*c*) All this obviously without excluding the need for serious *political involvement*, committed to liberating work from the forms of alienation derived from the dominant consumeristic and productivistic logic. An authentic ethics of work cannot do without an attitude which seriously questions these social systems, which determine or favour increasing enslavement in the world of work, economic and social imbalance and ecological deterioration at all levels. This is why it is vitally important to create the conditions to overcome the dissociation which still exists between spiritual life and real social life; above all it is necessary to move in the direction of an ethics which confronts the conflicts in this world and takes on the struggle to reform structures, so that everyone has the kind of work which is a free and creative vocation. Work is an inextricable tangle of liberation and alienation. It is one of the privileged places where man is called to exercise the difficult task of harmonising the conflicts of his life, in search of a unity which must be constructed together till its fulfilment at the last day.

Translated by Dinah Livingstone

Notes

1. B. Franklin is the most representative exponent of this tendency. In his list of virtues, temperance, by which is meant saving, and silence as activistic pragmatism, come first, whereas justice and humility come much later: see *Autobiography* (New Haven 1964; London 1970).

2. On certain aspects of the changing nature of industrial work, see A. Casciolli *Assenteismo e alienazione* (Milan 1979[2]); L. Frey *La problematica del lavoro giovanile e le sue prospettive negli anni 80* (Milan 1980); E. Minerva *L'assenteismo operaio. Ricerca empirica in una grande industria di base* (Milan 1980).

3. For an approach to the debate on the work crisis, both in the quantitative and the qualitative sense, in Italy see A. Accornero *Lavoro e non lavoro* (Bologna 1980); *idem. Il lavoro come ideologia* (Bologna 1980); F. Andolfi—M. Ingrosso—B. Manghi *Lavoro e non lavoro* (Milan 1980); *Lavoro: liberare il lavoro o liberarsi dal lavoro?* Supplement to no. 24 of *Il Manifesto*, 24 February 1981.

4. The classic text which attempted the first systematic treatment in theological terms is M. D. Chénu *The Theology of Work* (Dublin 1963).

5. M. D. Chénu 'La teologia cattolica e il lavoro' *IDOC Internazionale* nos. 5, 6, 7 (1980) pp. 46-47.

6. *Gaudium et Spes* §§ 34-39.

7. M. D. Chénu 'Lavoro' in *Dizionario Teologico* (Brescia 1967) II pp. 146-147.

8. See G. Campanini 'Lavoro' in *Diz. Enc. Teol. Mor.* (Rome 1976) pp. 502-503.

9. G. Angelinin 'Lavoro' in *Nuovo Dizionario di Teologia* (Rome 1977) pp. 723-724.

10. F. Totaro 'Il lavoro fra esigenza di umanizzazione e cultura del rifiuto' in *Quaderni di Azione Social* 5 (1979) pp. 53-54.

PART II

Questions from the Third World to the 'Christian West'

Walter Fernandes/Alfred de Souza

Work and Unemployment: What is Specific to the Third World?

TO BEGIN this paper by giving unemployment figures for India or any other developing country would be missing the point because the nature both of work and of unemployment is qualitatively, not merely quantitatively different in the Third World.

1. WORK AND UNEMPLOYMENT IN THE THIRD WORLD

(*a*) The predominance of the private sector

The major characteristic of employment in the Third World is the predominance of the informal (or unorganised) sector. According to the Government of India *Employment Review*, January-March 1981, in March 1981 only 22·92 million of 260 million active population or less than 10 per cent of the work force was in the organised sector.

Moreover, most of the work force is in the rural areas and nearly 70 per cent in the agricultural sector. Most other characteristics of the Third World working conditions are determined by the predominance of the informal sector and agricultural labour. The cities certainly face a major problem of slums and housing and unemployment in the formal and informal sectors, but the urban influx is conditioned by the employment situation in the rural areas. A major technical change in agriculture, as for example mechanisation that formed part of the Green Revolution, can render agricultural labourers jobless and create a push effect towards the urban slums. As a result, any solution of the problem of unemployment lies in creating more jobs in the informal sector and not in the organised sector.

This difference between the industrialised and Third World countries, is related to differences in their economic systems. As a recent study (Bairoch 1973: 10-11) shows, towards the end of the eighteenth century, consequent upon the industrial revolution and colonialism, Europe ceased to be an importer of manufactured goods especially from Asia and began to export them to its colonies. As far as the colonies were concerned,

> the large-scale importation of manufactured goods led to a drop in local production, since domestic consumption increased far more slowly than imports. Consequently,

in the manufacturing sector there was a fall in employment that was aggravated by the increase in productivity (albeit still fairly small) resulting from the use of more advanced techniques.

The same study suggests that, because of disease control in the newly independent countries and the consequent decline in mortality rates, there is a population inflation and as a result agricultural employment in the developing countries has reached its optimum level. However, since the colonial economic order continues, creation of jobs in the secondary sector is insufficient to cope with the annual increase in the active population which is estimated to grow at the rate of 2·4 per cent annually in Asia and Africa and 2·6 per cent in Latin America. In other words, the question of unemployment and the nature of work in the Third World is closely linked to the neo-colonial international economic order.

(b) Underemployment and low levels of income

Another feature of the employment pattern in the Third World as a whole is underemployment and low levels of income. A large proportion of the rural population is employed for only six months a year. But even during these months, their income is very low and insufficient to maintain their families. The months without work may mean starvation. Hence more jobs alone will not solve the problems of the Third World, but jobs with more income.

Lack of income itself is the result of an unfair distribution of assets in the poor countries. Reforming the international economic order is essential but not enough because what is true at the international level is equally true of the national scene. In South Asia landlessness is a major cause of poverty and inequality in its distribution is glaring. According to World Bank (1980: 41-42), 53 per cent of rural households in Bangladesh, 40 per cent in India and 86 per cent in Pakistan and similar proportions in Sri Lanka and Nepal were landless in 1978. Though India is the world's tenth most industrialised nation, the 1981 census estimates that 48 per cent of the country's population lives below the poverty (i.e., subsistence) line as against 40 per cent in 1961 (Dandekar and Rath 1971: 18-21).

For those living below the poverty line, employment is not a question of convenience but of survival. These are the most vulnerable sections of the population, and are the most affected by any change in the agricultural scene. The Green Revolution, for example, led to 'self-sufficiency' in food production in India and in 1977 the government had accumulated a buffer stock of 22 million tons of cereals. However, during the same year it was estimated that nearly 40 per cent of the Indian population was undernourished. The major reason for this situation is that the rural poor simply lack purchasing power. As a result, higher production need not necessarily lead to higher consumption by the poor.

(c) Lack of Social Security

Another distinctive feature of the employment pattern in the Third World is the total lack of social security in the informal sector. Benefits such as pension, provident fund, medical insurance and other schemes are available only to the small section in the organised sector. Moreover, unemployment benefits are totally unavailable in most countries of the Third World. Consequently, for the landless rural population unemployment is another word for starvation.

A major result of this situation is rural indebtedness. The landless who are unable to survive because of their low income, are forced to borrow money at inflated rates of interest from moneylenders since banks do not consider them creditworthy. Any emergency such as sickness or death or social events such as marriage only increases this indebtedness. Since they do not have any other permanent assets, they mortgage their only possession, i.e., their work. Bonded labour has thus become part of the rural scene in India and many Third World countries during a century of commercialisation of agricultural products. In many cases this bondage may continue over generations.

Besides, because of both bondage and the low income, children are forced to work sometimes even from the age of five. Among the weakest sections of the Indian population, even the income earned at this age may be essential for the survival of the family (Banerjee 1982: 128-130).

(*d*) Women in this system of labour

Women are another exploited category of this system of labour. A salaried job is accepted as a necessity or as normal by the urban middle class, but the weaker sections do not have a choice. Often women are forced to work outside and usually they get the hardest and the lowest paid work. However, women find it necessary to go and work since usually their wages are essential for the survival of the family.

What should be noted is that in most Asian countries the Worker Participation Rate (WPR) among women is very low. In India it is around 25 per cent and in no state does it exceed 30 per cent. However, among the poorer sections it exceeds 50 per cent and among the poorest it is more than 70 per cent (Gulati 1975: 38-40). This may be viewed by some as a sign of greater freedom among these women but is in reality a necessity. Similar studies in other Third World countries show a clear link between female exploitation and their WPR.

Besides, while even in the informal sector a proportionately larger number of men are engaged in semi-skilled jobs such as masonry, women are engaged mostly in unskilled jobs. In the rural areas they are mostly agricultural labourers who do strenuous work such as rice planting.

Even when women do what is considered less strenuous jobs, their work often becomes a mode of exploitation. Often they do contract jobs such as *beedi* (Indian cigarette) making or what is called the 'putting out' system. It is the system in which women in the informal sector undertake at home different kinds of work for industries in the formal sector. There is great exploitation in this system because the women are low-paid but cannot demand better wages since they are not organised and many other women would be prepared to take their place if some refused to participate.

To an extent, the question of withdrawing from the labour market is not realistic for women in low income groups because their earnings are used not for 'extras' but to meet the basic needs of the family—food, clothing, health (de Souza 1978: 21).

(*e*) The Caste System

Another discriminatory factor in employment is the hereditary nature both of the disabilities and of the low-status jobs because of the caste system. A very large section of those who belong to the informal sector and live in the urban slums or are rural landless agricultural labourers are persons belonging to what are called 'low castes' or the tribals. The low castes are victims of what is called 'cumulative inequality'. While 48 per cent of the total population of India lives below the poverty line, their proportion among the 'low castes' and tribals is estimated to be 80 per cent. More than 90 per cent of the bonded labourers in India belong to these groups. The WPR is extremely high among all age-groups of this section. In 1961, the WPR for the 5-14 age-group among them was estimated at 20 per cent and for the 60+ group at 61 per cent (Rayappa and Grover 1980:

51-53). In other words, these groups are malnourished in their infancy, begin to work in their childhood, are underpaid and lack job security in their adulthood and have to continue in the labour market as long as they physically can.

(*f*) The Rural-Urban Migration

Urban unemployment has to be viewed within the context of the exploitative situation in the rural areas and the unjust international economic order which deprives the Third World countries of the possibility of creating more urban jobs. Bairoch (1973: 26-39) gives three main reasons for rural-urban migration, the growth of slums and what he calls 'over-unemployment' in the Third World cities. There is the rapid growth of the rural population because of disease-control and saturation of the rural labour market causes the 'push' effect. The gap between urban and rural incomes, even in the informal sector and higher status attached to life in the cities, even in its slums, brings about the 'pull' effect attracting rural migrants. The urban-rural difference in income was more than 150 per cent in most Latin American countries, as much as 530 per cent in Venezuela, over 300 per cent in most African countries and over 100 per cent in most Asian countries in 1971. Added to this is the rapid increase in the literacy rates and the unreformed system of education that was geared to the needs of colonial administration and not meant for a country seeking to develop its industries or productive capacity.

Moreover, any major technical change and 'development' of the countryside may in fact have an adverse effect on the weaker sections, particularly women. Such is the case, for example, with the much-lauded Green Revolution which led to the migration of the traditional village blacksmiths and landless agricultural labourers to the cities where they were absorbed in the exploitative informal sector and the slums. Most of those who join this exploitative system are persons belonging to what are called 'low castes' or tribals. While these groups form about 19 per cent of India's population and 14·2 per cent of the urban population, they compromise about 65 per cent of the slum dwellers.

In other words, when we talk about rural-urban migration in India, the chances are high that the migrant will be from a low caste or an untouchable one, and will end up living in a slum or squatter settlement when he/she reaches the city (Singh 1978: 329).

2. SOME ETHICAL QUESTIONS

The major differences between the western and Third World in working conditions and unemployment raises several important ethical issues related to the present unjust international economic order.

(*a*) Overpopulation in the Third World or over-opulency in the industrialised countries?

The first question concerns the unwillingness of the industrialised countries to face the issue of injustice in the global economy by attributing poverty in the Third World to overpopulation. This position attributes poverty to the 'irrational reproductive habits' of the poor in the Third World.

This neo-Malthusian stance evades the basic issue of poverty as a consequence of the social, economic and political structures of society. Most studies have shown that people are not poor because they have many children but they have many children because they are poor. High infant mortality and relatively low life expectancy are important consequences of poverty. In 1974, infant mortality in India was as high as 120 in the rural areas and 80 in the urban areas. It was as high as 64·1 in the 0-4 age-group in India though the national average for all age-groups was only 19·1 per thousand. Moreover, studies have shown that the fertility rate among the poor has not come down because infant mortality as well as adult morbidity is much higher among them than among the upper social strata. In fact, studies of the construction workers in Delhi report high infant mortality rates indicating that 40-44 per cent of the children born had died (Singh and de Souza 1976: 101).

Thus, both at the national and international level, the present economic order is loaded against the poor and affects not only employment but the total quality of life and survival right from birth. In the present international economic system, 6 per cent of the world's population living in North America consumes 40 per cent of its resouces. In 1978 when the world's population was estimated at 4·4 billion, the world's greatest gross GNP was $8·5 trillion. This should have given a world *per capita* income of $2,000. However, in practice more than $7 trillion, i.e., roughly 80 per cent of this income was generated in the rich countries of North America and Europe that have 25 per cent of the world's population, thus giving them a *per capita* income of $6,000 and $500 for the remaining 75 per cent of the population (Demeny 1981: 280-281).

(*b*) Migrant Workers in the Industrialised Countries

The industrialised countries are becoming more conscious of the presence of migrant workers in all sectors of the economy. In some countries like Great Britain, mass migration was a consequence of British colonial policy which controlled its direction and flow. It would be mistaken to think that migrants from India and other countries of Asia to Great Britain and other European countries are part of what is called the 'brain drain'; on the contrary, a high proportion of Asian migrants to Great Britain, for example, particularly those from India, Pakistan and Bangladesh are illiterate and belong to the most disadvantaged sections of society. This flow of Asian migrants to Great Britain and elsewhere was responsive to the conditions of unemployment and currently the Gulf countries are replacing Britain and other European countries as the new hope for the unemployed. The situation of Asian migrant workers raises several ethical questions involving human rights, human dignity and the right to work. Racial discrimination may often be an expression of the unwillingness to extend to ethnic groups different from one's own the same claims to social, economic and job opportunities.

(*c*) Working Class in the Industrialised Countries and Workers in the Third World

Related to the question of Asian migrant workers in the industrialised countries is the question of solidarity of the working class which often tends to be self-centred and unconcerned about the consequences for workers in Third World countries. In the current situation of global interdependence, protectionism in the industrial or agricultural sector, because of lobbying power of the trade unions, may restrict the capacity of Third World countries to create new employment opportunities. Thus, for instance, the textile, steel and engineering industries which operate uneconomically and require massive government subsidies, function as so many barriers to manufactured goods from the developing countries which would have provided more employment. Thus worker solidarity in the industrialised countries operate with a national rather than a global perspective and their specific interests are assumed to represent the interests of all workers including those in the developing countries. This is no doubt a complex issue with considerable political significance, but increasingly it is being realised that the disparities between rich and poor countries and structural change in the international economic system will not occur unless an educational process of awareness spreads among the workers in the industrialised countries to make them conscious of their responsibilities to their underprivileged co-workers in Third World countries.

(*d*) Workers Subordinated to Work?

Unemployment in Third World countries and inequality of income distribution condemn millions of men, women and children to conditions of dehumanisation. When Pope Paul VI addressed the ILO on its 50th Anniversary, he made a moving statement that never again should the worker be subordinated to work but that work should be at the service of the worker. There has been a noticeable trend in the industrialised countries to humanise working conditions so that employment involves not merely economic rewards but also personal and psychological satisfaction. In the Third World where massive underemployment and employment is maintained by social and economic structures both national and international, workers are subordinated to work and this situation which deprives millions of their humanity is perhaps most clearly seen in bonded labour. It will not be possible for the urban and rural poor in the Third World to liberate themselves from bondage to work without the assistance of enlightened groups prepared to work both within and between nations to give primacy to man and the satisfaction of his basic human needs.

If a fuller utilisation of human resources is desired, employment will have to be accorded priority in national planning and international policy. When this happens the fundamental social purpose of economic development will emerge with the emphasis on human rights, social justice and freedom. This approach to the question of underemployment in the Third World poses a new challenge to the conscience of both the developing and developed countries to reorganise social, economic and political structures so that by meeting the basic needs of our common humanity, we may humanise the future.

References

Paul Bairoch *Urban Unemployment in Developing Countries* (Geneva 1973).

D. Banerji *Poverty, Class and Health Culture in India* (New Delhi 1982).

V. M. Dandekar and N. Rath *Poverty in India* (Bombay 1971).

Paul Demeny 'The North-South Income Gap: A Demographic Perspective' *Population and Development Review* 7 (1981) 297-310.

Alfred de Souza *Indian City* (New Delhi 1978).

Leela Gulati 'Female Work Participation: A Study of Inter-State Differences' *Economic and Political Weekly* 10 (1975) 25-42.

International Labour Organisation *Profile of Rural Poverty* (Geneva 1979).

H. P. Rayappa and D. Grover *Employment Planning for the Rural Poor* (Delhi 1980).

Andrea M. Singh and Alfred de Souza *Position of Women in Migrant Bastis in Delhi* (New Delhi 1976).

Andrea M. Singh 'Rural-Urban Migration of Women among the Urban Poor in India' *Social Action* 28 (1978) 326-356.

World Bank *World Development Report 1980* (Washington 1981).

José Beozzo

The Plight of Rural Workers in Brazil Today

'Worse than all the evils of work is the lack of work'—José Comblin

1. BEING A WORKER IN THE THIRD WORLD

If we take the sixteenth century and the present day as the two ends of an arc extending over the growth of 'modern times', during which the social and technical conditions of the organisation of labour we know today have been forged, two examples can serve to illustrate the progress made by workers in the Third World.

How was it that the very modernity which in the sixteenth century saw the destruction of the feudal system and the end of the 'glebe servant', with the coming of the 'free' worker in British manufacture, also produced the destruction of the free Indians of America and saw the rise of the 'assigned' Indian in the mines of Mexico and Peru, and the enslaved African on the sugar plantations of north-eastern Brazil? What a strange phenomenon, to produce such contradictory historical outcomes at the same time! and how was it that the same people and nations who wrote the sagas of the struggles for liberation in the eighteenth century, with their cries of 'Liberty, Equality, Fraternity', were also implacable overlords and defenders of colonial tyranny in the Americas?

Or how was it that European Christianity could split so irrevocably into Catholics and Protestants at home, and yet come together harmoniously to 'reduce' indigenous populaces to forced labour, to set up the traffic in negro slaves and to organise slave labour in the lands of America? Could anyone tell the difference between the business set up by a pious Dutch Calvinist in the Antilles from that established by a nobleman from Catholic Spain on the island of Cuba, or that set up by an Anglican gentleman, most faithful subject of his Brittanic majesty, in Jamaica, or that run by a Portuguese Catholic in Pernambuco, or by a representative of the *'fille ainée de l'Eglise'* in the French possessions of Haiti or Martinique? Now could they, when the marks of them all were the overseer's whip, the naked torsos of the slaves, the cries of the tortured and the whole cruel apparatus of slavery?

How was it that the same system could at the same time require free workers in the 'centre' (the Old World) and produce slave labour on the 'periphery' (the New World)?

Coming to the present day, we find that despite the illusion that the German worker on the Volkswagen assembly line at Wolfsburg is carrying out the same function as his Brazilian colleague at 'Volks' in São Bernardo do Campo, both producing the same end product, with the same brand name and the same technical specifications, through the same administrative machinery and reaching virtually identical grades of productivity, in fact the same extraordinary inequality of the past is reproduced on a different level. The same can be said of the other multinationals and their subsidiaries—in the automobile industry, in chemical process, in electric power. A comparative table of wage earnings in different countries will show what it means to do the same job in the First and Third Worlds:

Wages paid by Ford in 1981

Country	*US $ per hour*
United States/Canada	10·5
Spain	4·5
Mexico	4·5
Argentina	3·2
Venezuela	3·0
Brazil	1·0

Source: International Metal Workers' Federation in Latin America, *Weekly Report* 81.03, 16 January 1981.

Note: Due to differences in methods of collecting information, figures are estimates.[1]

The table shows clearly why the multinationals are so keen to transfer their operations to certain countries in the Third World, where labour is abundant, where there are no trade unions, where strong governments undertake to disrupt and repress workers' movements, where there are no anti-pollution laws, no anti-trust laws, where working codes of practice and employers' contributions are practically non-existent, where there are all sorts of tax loopholes, and, above all, where the wage levels are such that in Europe or the United States they would be unable to attract even the most needy immigrant worker, such as Turks, Moroccans, Portuguese or Spaniards in the Common Market, or Mexicans without papers in the United States. Given the differences in working conditions in the past and the present, it can be seen that capitalism, which in Europe came with the end of feudal servitude, monarchic despotism and religious obscurantism, proclaiming an age of enlightenment, of freedom and equality, cannot make the same claims in Latin America. Here capitalism does not look for arguments in favour of freedom, but for those that enable it to enslave people.

So the critique that can be made of modern systems, whether capitalist or socialist, is of the civilisation they are both building, which is already present in the dawning 'work society' in Latin America, which is virtually one based on slave labour.

The same criticism was made in the early days of this society, by the 'assigning' cleric Bartolomé de Las Casas, who was converted in Cuba in 1514, through meditating on Chapter 34 of Ecclesiasticus, verses 20-22, and applying them to the situation of the Indians reduced to slavery that he himself was exploiting:

Offering sacrifice from the property of the poor
    is as bad as slaughtering a son before his father's very eyes.
A meagre diet is the very life of the poor,
    he who withholds it is a man of blood.

A man murders his neighbour if he robs him of his livelihood,
sheds blood if he withholds an employee's wages.[2]

In Latin America, criticism of the work society began to be made in the name of the poor, the root and principle of all criticism, the poor who in Latin America were the Indians, driven off their land, deprived of their political and social organisation, their language and their religion, reduced finally to the condition of slaves so that they could be put to work not for themselves and their families but for the European colonisers; so that they had to abandon work designed to ensure their survival to take up work designed to ensure an ever-increasing supply of gold and silver to the conquerors. The nerve centre of this civilisation was well and truly identified by an indigenous *cacique* of Peru, who said: 'The God of the Spaniards is gold'.

The same conscience impelled Fray Antonio de Montesinos, when he preached in Cuba in 1511: 'Tell me, by what right and with what justice do you hold these Indians in such cruel and horrible slavery? . . . How can you keep them so oppressed and exhausted, giving them nothing to eat, without treating the illnesses they incur from the excessive work you impose on them, so that they die on you, or rather, you kill them, just to mine and acquire gold every day?'[3]

Las Casas went on to say that it was only the greed of the conquistadors to acquire riches that killed the Indians. He saw that it was not so much personal evil intentions as the ineluctable result of the system implanted in the New World that led the Indians to their death: 'I do not say that you wish to kill them directly, out of any hatred you might feel for them, but that you want to be rich and have an abundance of gold, which is your only aim, through the labour and sweat of the afflicted and anguished Indians, using them as means and dead instruments, from which follows, of necessity, the death of all of them'.[4]

Their death followed of necessity from the system of forced labour imposed on the Indians in the building of a new social order designed not to satisfy material needs and ensure the survival of the workers, but to ensure indefinite accumulation of wealth. The pretext for this new order was often the proclamation of the Gospel to the Amer-indians. Las Casas would not countenance this use of religion to cover colonial exploitation and a social order based on gold: 'since Christ did not do this; he did not come into the world to die for gold, but to suffer for men so as to save men'.[5]

So Las Casas, faced with the refined and malicious use of the missionary pretext to obtain exploitation of Indian labour and the sought-after gold, daringly said that the glory of God was not to be found in the Indian baptised and condemned to death through the exploitation of his labour, but in the live Indian, even if pagan. It was this defence of *life*, human and material life, which was not to be deceitfully mutilated and exploited in the interests of a future, spiritual life, that lay at the root of all Las Casas' criticism of the colonial system: '. . . the Indians should be taken away from the Christians and set free'.[6] His main argument was that, 'although they may gain nothing in their souls, at least they would gain in life, and in multiplication on earth; which is less bad than losing everything'.[7]

Historical demography is now shedding light on the unheard-of destruction and death which the conquest and the reduction of the Indians to forced labour in the mines and the fields produced in Latin America: the population of Mexico, for example, estimated at 16·8 million in 1532, in the early years of the conquest, was reduced to 1·8 million by 1580, fifty years later.[8]

So it was in the name of the poor, in the name of life itself and the survival of the poor, that criticism was made in the past of the European colonial enterprise in Latin America, which was mounted on labour reduced to slavery, on exploitation without limit or restriction.

2. BEING A WORKER IN BRAZIL TODAY

More than in any other country of Latin America, the history of labour in Brazil cannot be separated from the stamp put on it by slavery, since this was the country where most African slaves were brought: between 3·5 and 3·6 million before 1850, the date of the abolition of negro slave traffic. This represents some 38 per cent of all the slaves brought to the New World.[9]

Brazil was also the last country in the whole of America to abolish slave labour, in 1888. In Haiti, it was done in 1794, in Mexico in 1829, in the United States in 1865.

The result of this concentrated importation of African labour was that all productive work, along with all public works and all domestic service, was performed exclusively by slaves, who in some regions accounted for between 70 and even 90 per cent of the population. By the first quarter of the nineteenth century, the majority of the population of Brazil was made up of slaves. So a whole mentality grew up, in which work was for slaves, and considered unworthy of a free man or woman. Slaves worked under the strict control of an overseer and under the continual threat of the lash, or of crueller and more prolonged punishment.

The first task of the owner was to train the African who had just arrived from Angola, the Gold Coast or Guinea, teaching him his work, in a regime of captivity, along with the rudiments of the language necessary for him to understand his orders, and some basic elements of the Catholic religion, along with the virtues necessary to every slave: obedience, humility, fidelity. The way of violence was always at hand to subdue the proud or recalcitrant slave, to punish disobedience or insolence. The basic aim was to form a slave through persuasion of one sort or another so that he would work without the need for continual vigilance, and without risk of him revolting or being a threat to his owner's life or property. Religion played a fundamental part in obtaining the slave's submission to his lot. So his sufferings were made to have meaning and merit through the Passion of Christ, as was continually taught in sermons and homilies: 'There is no work or way of life more like the Cross and Passion of Christ than yours in one of these enterprises. Blessed are you if you can learn to understand the good fortune of your state, and through conforming to and imitating such a high and divine example, use it to sanctify your labour. In an enterprise you are imitators of Christ crucified, because you suffer in a way very similar to the way our Lord himself suffered on the Cross and in the whole of his Passion. . . . The Passion of Christ took place partly in a night without sleep, and partly in a day without rest, and such are your nights and days; Christ was despised and you are despised, Christ had no food and you go hungry, Christ was ill-treated in every way, and so are you. Irons, prisons, whips, chains, insults: all these make up your initiation, which, if patience goes with it, will also have the merit of martyrdom. . . . When you serve your masters, do not serve them as you would men, but as one serves God; because then you are not serving as captives but as free men, you are not obeying as slaves but as sons.'[10]

What else but religion could put forward this supreme transfiguration, in which the slave-owner, who condemns his slaves to hard labour and hopeless servitude, has to be served like God himself, and in which the slave, in serving, feels like a free man and a son before the Father?

Religion was trying to bring conciliation to a world of harsh opposites, peace in the midst of antagonistic work relationships, harmony in a world of punishment and violence, proposing the precepts of love to both slaves and masters and to each the virtues proper to their station: benevolence on the part of the master, submission for the slave; moderation to the former, patience to the latter, firmness in correction and kindness in punishing to the master, continuous application to work and grateful acceptance on the part of the slave. Moralists like Jorge Benci, a Jesuit of the late eighteenth century, set themselves the Herculean task of working out a system of morality applicable to 'a Christian economy of masters in the government of slaves', even while recognising that, 'the servant works and the master reaps the fruit of his labour. Can there be a more lamentable state of affairs? . . . One day goes by and another; months pass, and years; and the poor slaves work on, without comfort, without rest, without respite; in the sun and the rain; without sleeping at night and without stopping by day. And the fruits and profits from all this work, who is it that enjoys them and consumes them? Not them, but others; not the slaves themselves, but their masters. . . .'[11]

This is why work is a curse for the slave, whereas leisure is the good he most desires, more even than his own freedom. But ninety years of 'free' work in Brazil have not been enough to rid the ruling classes in the country of the habits inherited from the slave owners, a mixture of paternalism and authoritarianism, benevolence and harshness in their treatment of employees.

Though there were followers of the tradition of Las Casas in Brazil who fought for the freedom of the Indians, there was nothing similar in relation to the negro slaves. The dominant theology by the end of the nineteenth century was not one of liberation, but one of slavery, a theology and a morality designed to form the virtues of a 'master' and those of a slave, in their respective hearts.

The transition from slave to 'free' labour came about with the shift from African to European immigrant workers: Italians took the place of African slaves on the coffee plantations of São Paulo, particularly from 1870 onwards. Semi-slave workers, weighed down by the cost of the journey, which had to be paid for by four or five years work, they were also permanently in debt to the plantation stores, from which they were obliged to purchase their clothes, food and working tools.

In just a few places in Brazil, work stopped being a curse and became a blessing: in a few places in the South where a limited number of immigrants (around 3 per cent of the total of 4·5 million European immigrants who came into the country between 1870 and 1930) were allowed to buy small plots of land which they could cultivate. Here the ground watered with the sweat of the immigrant's brow could produce fruits for him and his family that were not immediately taken away from them to the profit of someone else. Here was born a different class of humanity from the battered, humiliated, suffering, alienated humanity of the rest of rural Brazil.

3. THE RURAL WORKER: FROM SETTLER AND PEASANT TO PEON AND 'COLD-SNACKER'

So we come to the situation for the rural workers today. They form a contingent of some 40 million landless workers, in a country which is sparsely populated and has enormous areas of apparently available land: barely 4 per cent of cultivatable land area is worked. Most of these 40 million work on other people's land under various forms of contract: either for a parcel of rented land or for a wage only, which is becoming the usual form, with the increasing penetration of the capitalist system into the country. Around 700,000 families occupy lands in the regions furthest from consumer markets and most lacking in means of communication, as *posseiros* (smallholders), families who live on a small piece of land handed down to them, from which they eke out a subsistence living.

Besides the mass of those who have no land, the minority who possess some are clearly divided into two classes. On one hand, the smallholders whose properties do not exceed ten hectares represent 52·3 per cent of rural establishments, occupying a mere 2·8 per cent of privately owned land; on the other, the big landowners with more than

1,000 hectares, represent only 0·8 per cent of properties, but occupy 42·6 per cent of the land.[12]

Brazil's timid labour legislation, started in the 1920s under pressure from the Treaty of Versailles, was approved by Parliament with the expressed caveat that it applied only to industrial workers in the towns and not to the workers in the country, where 70 per cent of the population lived. Rural workers went on being excluded from the legislation till 1963, when under pressure from the mobilisation of agricultural workers and the first rural unions, the Goulart government promulgated the Statute for Rural Workers. The gains from the mobilisation of the early Sixties were promptly wiped out by the military coup of 1964 which dealt harshly and repressively with the burgeoning unions, arrested, tortured and assassinated the leaders of the agricultural workers, and so restored the old 'order' to the country once again.

The response of the great landowners to the beginnings of labour legislation for rural workers, providing for a minimum wage, some form of security depending on the number of years worked and other minimal benefits, had been a massive expulsion of workers from their properties. These workers were then forced to camp in the shanty towns around the cities. They lived in the city, but every morning they were loaded into trucks like cattle and taken back to the estates to do their day's work without the protection of any sort of law. They became casual labourers, hired by a new employer, generally the owner of the truck, every day, and sent off to a different place of work. They lost any regular contract of employment, any right to paid rest times, any holidays, any medical assistance they might have had under the previous system. When it rained or they were sick, they got no money. If they had an accident at work, no one was responsible, since they had no fixed employer. In this way the new social legislation was stood on its head, and casual labour, virtually unknown twenty years ago, now accounts for seven million rural workers, whose labour is bought outside the bounds of any legislation, beyond the laws of the most primitive form of capitalism.

This was the vengeance of the great landowners who could exploit the work force, while relieving themselves of any corresponding social cost. Their workers, known as '*boia-frias*' ('cold-snackers'), because they took with them a little rice and beans which they had to eat cold at midday, had no proof of employment other than the callouses on their hands. They have had to struggle till now for recognition by the union for rural workers, so that their medical expenses could be met; they are now fighting for better transport and for some way to ensure that their miserable pay—some $2·5 for a ten-hour day or longer for men, 75 per cent of this sum for women and 50 per cent for children—keeps pace with galloping inflation. When the harvests are finished, or in times of drought, they hang around the roads out of the cities, trying to find a job for the day. Few do, and they end up by sending their children into the city to beg for food.

While in the South of the country the former coffee plantation workers are becoming 'cold-snackers', a different change is taking place in the North, in the 5·5 million square kilometres that make up Amazonia: the transformation of the smallhoders and all those who lived by selling materials from the forest into peons of the great cash crop enterprises. Word went out from the government in 1967 to 'occupy' Amazonia, as though it had not already been occupied—by the remnants of the indigenous population (200,000 people), by the colonisation of the seventeenth century, by the gold rush of the eighteenth, by an exodus from the North-East in the nineteenth, and by the thousands of labourers who have moved there to plant a few crops and live in peace away from the exploitation of the landowners. 'Occupying' Amazonia meant taking it over through the capital of the multinationals, the great commercial and industrial enterprises of the South of the country, the banks. The old agrarian capital, whose exports had been the base of all Brazil's accumulated wealth, was thereby reinforced with new commercial and financial capital. Any company investing in land in Amazonia could claim a 50 per cent tax rebate, as well as virtually interest-free loans from the government, for mining projects, timber felling and, the most popular, stock rearing. So any company could carve out a huge empire for itself, using public funds: the Rockefeller Corporation bought 531,000 hectares in Mato Grosso, the Italian Liquigás group bought out Suiá-Missu, with 577,000 hectares in the Araguaia region; Volkswagen set up in the Valle do Rio Cristalino, with 100,000 head of cattle on a plot of 139,640 hectares. National Bulk Carriers own 1,250,000 hectares in Pará, and Georgian Pacific 400,000. In Minas Gerais, Brazilian Land Packing owns 2,913,696 hectares, an area almost the size of Belgium.[13] In the Amapá region the biggest landowner is the Bethlehem Steel Corporation, and there too, the ambitious Jari project was undertaken by the American Daniel Ludwig, covering an area the size of Holland, in the hands of a single owner. Despite the Constitution, which protects indigenous lands, and the Land Statute of 1964, which protects the rights of smallholders, the companies have been able to obtain fraudulent 'negative certificates' declaring that there are no Indians or smallholders on the land, and so systematically expel Indians and smallholders from the areas they have acquired.

One can ask what motivates these companies, who own vast tracts of land, of which only a few hundred hectares have in fact been cultivated, to undertake this systematic expulsion, by fraud, pressure, violence and even assassination, of Indians and smallholders from their land? What harm are the smallholders, with their two or three hectares each on which they just manage to support their families, doing them?

It is the same drive that led the first colonisers to expel the Indians from their lands in order to set up their exploitative enterprises, hunting down the Indians hiding in the bush to drag them back to the same lands, no longer as free workers producing for themselves, but as slaves, producing for the benefit of their exploiters.

In these distant parts with sparse population, the smallholders are the only available labour force; while they have their freedom and can support themselves, they are not going to sell their labour. So all the land has to be occupied so that there is none available; the owners have to be expelled, their crops burned, and then they are brought back, no longer as owners of that same piece of land, but as wage earners in the service of the estate, as peons looking after the herds on the big pastures. The work they had as a blessing when they owned their own land has been turned into a curse.

As an illustration of this bloody struggle going on over the whole of the interior of Brazil, here is a deposition made by the smallholders of the Prelazia de Marabá in southern Pará:

> Highway PA-70, which links the Pará city of Marabá with Brasilia, crosses the area which we had chosen as our new home and the future patrimony of our children. In 1965, when the PA-70 was a narrow service road, we arrived and set ourselves up between km 40 and km 92 where, in the middle of virgin forest, we paid heed to the government's appeal and set about clearing the land to produce more food for the country.
>
> At that time, government propaganda declared that the government was conscious of the plight of the poor people of Brazil, particularly in areas where land was being turned over from cultivation to stock rearing. That more and more cereals had to be produced to feed the growing population of Brazil. We came here and we produced. We want nothing except to work—not just to survive each day, but to build up a patrimony, to have economic independence, so that one day we can have something to call our own that we have produced with our individual labour. But after all that effort to tame the virgin land, there appear 'landowners' to claim our services, our homes, our pieces of land. This is not just. Many of us were expelled, pressed into labour, humiliated. Many lost all they possessed. We have been the

losers from the start in this struggle. It is against this that we are rising up in the hope of receiving justice, and demanding of the authorities: *Sirs, we only want what is ours! We want the right to work and live with dignity on the land we cultivated with the sweat of our brows.*'[14]

In the South, the expulsion of those who worked the land and its concentration into the hands of a few businesses and landowners has provided the basis for transforming the labourers into 'cold-snackers', while the smallholders of the North have been turned into peons on the cattle ranches, all forced to sell their labour at rock-bottom prices, swelling the ranks of those who have been dispossessed of their land and humiliated in their dignity as workers.

4. THE CHURCH AND LAND PROBLEMS

Except in the Jesuit reductions in Paraguay (1610-1768), where the Church helped the Guaranis to defend their lands against the bands of brigands who came to capture meek Indians to sell them as slave labour in the sugar plantations, it has not paid much attention to land problems. It has itself been part of the colonial system, with large properties and businesses of its own. Even the Jesuits were implicated in this, and their estates were models of organisation and lucrative businesses for the owners of the time.

In Brazil, the first document to tackle the question of agrarian reform was a letter by the Bishop of Campanha, Don Inocencio Engelke, in 1950. In 1963, the National Bishops' Conference, in the midst of the controversy over the Basic Reform project put forward by the Goulart government, lent its support to these reforms, which included agrarian reform. Needless to say, it was land, the basis of all traditional power in Brazil, that was one of the direct causes of the fall of the Goulart government in 1964. This was followed by a renewed silence on the part of the Church, broken in 1971 by the courageous voice of Don Pedro Casaldáliga, Bishop of São Felix do Araguaia, in his first pastoral letter, whose title goes to the heart of the problem: 'A Church of Amazonia in conflict with large estates and social marginalisation', and whose opening words defined the new bishop's mission: 'If a bishop's first mission is to be a prophet, and if a prophet is one "who tells the truth before the whole people"; if being a bishop means being the voice of those who have no voice, then I can honestly no longer keep my mouth shut now that I have received the fullness of the priestly mission of service.'[15]

The whole letter is a powerful description of the invasion of Amazonia by the forces of capitalism, of the expulsion and massacre of the Indians and smallholders, with the government turning a blind eye, and the connivance of magistrates, local governors, judges and land registry offices, and the corruption of the officers of the National Foundation for the Indians and the National Institute for Settlement and Agrarian Reform, with the support of the police and the army.

The work situation in the country was also acutely analysed and strongly denounced in two other Church documents: 'Marginalisation of a People' by the Bishops of the Centre East, and 'I Heard the Cries of my People', by the Bishops of the North West, both produced in 1972, during the worst period of the Medici dictatorship. The Pastoral Land Commission has produced extensive studies on the whole vast and complex problem area of land over the whole country, so enabling the Church to act with increasing coherence and relevance.

The hundreds of disputes over land, where the Church has been present in one way or another—through pastoral agents, members of the base communities, Christian militants in the unions, or the presence of bishops and priests standing between the forces of the police or the army and unarmed workers—have led the Church of Brazil to the solemn commitment taken on at its General Assembly in February 1980, in the document: 'The Church and land problems'. This commitment can be summed up in the following points:

(i) Church lands and property to be submitted to a new examination to decide their pastoral and social use.
(ii) Overtly unjust situations and instances of violence in the country to be openly denounced, and their causes opposed.
(iii) Support to be given to workers' initiatives and organisations, placing the strengths and means of the Church at their service.
(iv) Support to be given to country people's efforts at agrarian reform, defending or promoting programmes for family ownership, for tribal property in the Indian areas, for community holdings in which land is regarded as an asset to be worked. Support to be given equally to mobilising workers to demand the implementation and/or reform of existing laws, so as to achieve a policy for land ownership, working practices and social security that will meet the needs of the population.[16]

The main novelty of this Church document consists in its assimilation of the viewpoint of the oppressed rural classes, based on the distinction between exploitative land and working land:

'Exploitative land is land where capital is used to create continual growth, to produce ever-increasing profits. These profits can come from the exploitation of the labour of those who have been dispossessed of their land and instruments of work, or from that of those who never had these; also from speculation, which allows a few to get rich at the expense of the whole of society.

Working land is land owned by those who work it. It is not for exploiting the labour of others, nor for speculation. In our country, the concept of working land is strongly entrenched in the popular right to family, tribal and community property. These forms of ownership, alternatives to capitalist exploitation, clearly open up a broad way to achieving community work, even over wide areas, with the utilisation of proper technology, making the exploitation of the labour of others unnecessary.

There is in the country a clear opposition between two regimes of ownership: on the one hand the regime which leads to conflict with agricultural labourers—capitalist ownership; on the other, those alternative forms of ownership mentioned above, which are being destroyed or mutilated by capital. . . .'[17]

In its strong condemnation of exploitative land and its approval instead of the use and possession of land on the basis of work, the document anticipates the position of *Laborem Exercens* in its statements on property and ownership of the means of production: 'These cannot be owned against labour, nor can they be owned simply for the sake of ownership, since the only legitimate title to their ownership is . . . that they be used for work. Consequently, by serving for work, the first principle of that order, which is that goods are for all and all have a right to their use, can be put into effect' (LE 14).

These remarks on rural labour can be concluded with another passage from *Laborem Exercens* which deals with working conditions in objectively unjust situations: 'In certain developing countries, there are millions of men who are forced to cultivate land belonging to others, with no hope that they can one day possess even the tiniest parcel of land "as their own". There are no forms of legal protection for the person of the agricultural worker or for his family. . . . Long days of hard physical labour are miserably paid. Cultivatable land is left idle or abandoned by the proprietors; legal titles to possession of a small piece of land, cultivated for years by those who live on it, are overruled or prove worthless in the face of the "land hunger" of more powerful individuals or groups' (LE 21).

Translated by Paul Burns

Notes

1. IBASE *Dossie sobre Emprego no. 1* (Rio de Janeiro, 10.8.81) p. 14 (roneo'd).
2. E. Dussel *Historia de la Iglesia en America Latina—Coloniaje y liberación—1492-1973* (Barcelona 1974) p. 92.
3. B. de Las Casas *Historia de las Indias* in 'Selected Works' (Madrid 1957-1958) II p. 176.
4. *Ibid.* V p. 89.
5. *Ibid.* V p. 88.
6. 'Carta de Vice-provincial (Fray Pedro de Córdoba) y sacerdotes del convento de Santo Domingo. dirijida a los muy reverendos padres' in *Libro Anual* (Mexico 1974) p. 160.
7. *Ibid.*
8. Dussel, in the work cited in note 2, p. 85. See C. W. Borah *The Indian Population of Central Mexico, 1531-1610* (California 1960) p. 48.
9. M. Bergmann *Nasce un povo* (Petrópolis 1977) p. 79.
10. K. de Q. Mattoso *Ser escravo no Brasil* (São Paulo 1982) pp. 114-115.
11. J. Benci *Economia cristã dos senhores no governo dos escravos* (São Paulo 1977) pp. 214-215.
12. CNBB *Igreja e Problemas de Terra* Estudos CNBB 17 (São Paulo 1980) p. 5.
13. *Pastoral da Terra: posse e conflitos* Estudos CNBB 13 (São Paulo 1976) pp. 176-177.
14. *Ibid.* p. 31.
15. P. Casaldáliga 'Uma Igreja na Amazōnia em conflito com o latifúndio e a marginalização social' in *Os documentos da CNBB: Igreja e Governo* in *Extra 3* I (February 1977) p. 37.
16. CNBB *Igreja e Problemas da Terra* pp. 33-35.
17. *Ibid.* pp. 30-31.

Ignacio Ellacuria

The Kingdom of God and Unemployment in the Third World

1. THE APPROACH TO THE QUESTION

UNEMPLOYMENT IS a structural problem because it is caused not only by human plans and choices but, above all, by economic and political systems which entail a larger or smaller proportion of the labour force remaining outside the labour market. Unemployment is an ethical problem because its causes and effects, as well as its remedies, have to do with human plans and choices, and unemployment deprives people of one of the most fundamental ways of fulfilling themselves. But unemployment is also a strictly theological problem because it involves God's will for his kingdom. Jesus came to proclaim, among other things, the historical effectiveness of the Father's kingdom among men, through the giving of the Son in the incarnation and his suffering even to death and through the gift of the Spirit to make all things new. But this kingdom of God even among men cannot be even minimally acceptable and credible in a situation in which a large part of humanity, especially the poorest, are deprived not only of the essentials for life but even of the possibility of keeping themselves alive and freely realising themselves.

If we approach unemployment from the point of view of the kingdom of God, it becomes a strictly theological problem because it tells us—by negation—something about God and because unemployment is a subject with which the word and action for the building of the kingdom of God as revealed in Jesus, is concerned. This theological character does not exclude the socio-economic character or the strictly ethical character of unemployment, both in the sphere of individual ethics and social and political ethics.

The Third World is a good place, perhaps the best place, to discover the theological character of unemployment. Of course we cannot ignore the importance of this social phenomenon in the First World, the western capitalist world. For example in the month of June 1982 in the United States, the economically strongest country in the western world, the predominant capitalist country, there were 10 per cent unemployed and this was the highest unemployment rate since the Second World War. This is of course a very important fact and says a great deal about things to do with man and the social structure. Moreover in the First World there are now millions of people who lack or are deprived of work which gives them a minimum of security and dignity.

However, even when we recognise this fact, it is only from the perspective of the

Third World that we can see what unemployment is in itself in its socio-economic significance and its ethical and theological meaning. Why is this? We do not need to resort to general principles which are also valid for this problem, such as that the Third World offers the greatest historical universality and, from the standpoint of Christian theology, it constitutes a theological place *par excellence* because it is formally a world of the poor. It is preferable and sufficient here to confine ourselves to the problem of unemployment itself and look at it in the Third World from the viewpoint of the kingdom of God.

In fact unemployment is a defining phenomenon of the Third World. What is a relatively marginal problem in the First World and a minor problem in the socialist world is in the Third World a problem not merely massive but consubstantial. So it is in the Third World that the problem stands out most clearly, even though subjective tolerance of it is greater in poor countries than in rich countries. And this is true even without stressing that the remedies proposed for unemployment in the First World can cause greater unemployment in the Third World. In general we can say that the ultimate truth and reality of many things which are done in the First World can only be discovered when we see their effects on the whole of humanity, a criterion which tends to be ignored not only by the strategists of world politics and economics but also by the makers of ethics and theology in the First World. But even prescinding from the fact that we cannot resolve unemployment in the First World by off-loading it onto the Third World, the unemployment which exists in the latter has certain peculiar characteristics. We mention only a few of them.

(a) Unemployment in the Third World is massive and chronic and is bound up with the economic order. These three facts are fundamental. Unemployment is not a problem which affects a few but a general problem; when it is not covered up it can affect half the potential working population. Unemployment is not occasional, because even though possible economic booms in capitalist countries bring unemployment down and even though the work of harvesting usually drastically lowers the unemployment rate for a few months, the truth is that a large part of the population is habitually unemployed or sub-employed. Finally unemployment is due largely to unequal conditions of exchange, which are consubstantial with the dominant world economic order.

(b) In the Third World there are no mechanisms to palliate the effects of unemployment. Whereas in the First World there are social security structures to help the unemployed, there are not and cannot be any in the Third World because employment is chronic and affects the majority. In El Salvador for example, only 5 per cent of the work force is urban industrial and they are the only ones to get social security. The State, for its part, has no other mechanisms to help the unemployed.

(c) Unemployment in the Third World is mainly a problem for people and families who live in the country and agricultural areas. It is possible in these areas to live with very few resources but on the other hand the unemployment leads to massive migrations to the cities.

(d) Unemployment affects families with many children and young people in their care. As a result, the young are forced into activities which makes them unable to obtain even a minimum of schooling and puts them in the worst possible educational conditions.

If we remember that this phenomenon is massive in the Third World and that the Third World represents easily three-quarters of humanity, radical conclusions follow. What humanity is this which allows and even requires this situation for the sake of a development from which so few benefit? How come there is such a lack of solidarity between people that this situation can be tolerated? What is this present economic order that it should require or permit such a monstrosity? What kingdom of God did Jesus come to proclaim to humanity? What price his beatitudes to the poor?

2. THEOLOGICAL REFLECTIONS ON UNEMPLOYMENT IN THE THIRD WORLD

(*a*) The sin of the world

Unemployment is one of the manifestations of what must be considered as the sin of the world, the sin of the world that Jesus came to take away. The sin of the world is the reality of this world and the people in it in negation and opposition to what God wanted of it when he created it and what he sought for it in the proclamation of the kingdom of God through the mouth of Jesus. A reality which profoundly and universally affects the majority of people in the world and its large-scale ordering, and which is moreover the negation of God among men, can very well be described as the sin of the world. Sin which is not just a pure ethical failing but the positive negation of God as Father, who wants his children to enjoy the inheritance that comes to them in the incarnate only-begotten Son and prevents them experiencing the Spirit poured out into their hearts so that they feel they are brothers and live as such. The sin of the world, which instead of disappearing increases its effects on the dispossessed and oppressed, a burden on them which is a terrible argument against the existence of a God who has revealed himself to us as Father and against the promise of the kingdom. How or why can this problem be resolved in the other world if we do not even begin to resolve it in this? Sin of the world also because it reduces our solidarity with one another and leads us to believe more in the idols of this world than in God revealed in Jesus. People who call themselves Christians and who nevertheless place their fulfilment, their security and their happiness in riches, power and ensuring that they have the first seats in religious services and practices. This allows them to pass by on one side the man who fell among robbers on the margin of history and preserve the privileges and advantages of the ecclesial institution. In return they offer the silence of complicity or a decaffeinated word.

And this is made worse because the First World calls itself Christian, the product of a Christian civilisation, the missionary of a Gospel which it took to the Third World as one more ingredient in its colonisation. It is possible that most of the unemployed in the western world and most of the unemployed in the Third World see not only the ineffectiveness of the Church's words but also the scandal of a Church which cares more about those that have than about those that are, more about those that have wealth and power than those that are God's favourite children to whom the promise of the kingdom was made first.

(*b*) Restoring the balance

In the face of this global sin what the Third World is asking for is conversion and transformation. Cultural, social and political movements inspired by opposition to the dominant power lead to radical transformations of the present economic structures; Christian or simply human forces which lead to conversion, not just of individuals who can do little, but of social groups and especially those social groups which are called nations. A change of mind and a change of historical direction.

We are not merely concerned with the fact that the dynamic which produces unemployment in the western world is then transferred to the Third World, although we know this happens. Or with the fact that just as the dynamic of unemployment is exported, the positive dynamic of development which has this negative effect of unemployment is also exported. It seems clear that not all countries can be rich countries and it also seems clear that in order for there to be rich countries, there must also be poor countries. We know that one of the ways to avoid conflict with the poorest people in one's own country is to export the causes of the conflict and to transfer the burden both at the point of work (upon primary materials) and at the point of buying exchange or consumer goods—outside one's own frontiers. Here we are concerned more profoundly with the creation not only of a new world economic order in which relations of exchange are more just, but of a new civilisation which is no longer built upon the pillars of hegemony and domination, accumulation and difference, consumption and false well being, but upon more human and Christian foundations. For as long as the rich countries refuse, in their international relations, to give up being hegemonic powers, and in their national systems, to give up having higher and lower standards of living, where 'higher' is ridiculously understood to mean more superfluity and conspicuous consumption, there are no solutions. Or there is no other solution than world revolution, which they try to suffocate in its most timid beginnings.

This may sound like Utopia, but a day will come when it will become a necessity to restore the imbalance between the disposable resources and the resouces required for galloping development in all spheres of life (except those of humanising culture, living convivially and openness to divine transcendence).

And it may also sound like Utopia to speak of the relativisation of the concept and feeling of nation. Fundamentally it is nonsense to feel ourselves more French, Japanese, North American or Chinese than human. Even though the problem is extremely complex and there is no sense in abdicating from the cultural wealth of different individual nationalities, this does not mean that humanity should be confined within purely national horizons. Nationalism apparently makes those who belong to a nation richer and more human, but this is through the sacrifice of higher values. That which is clear in science, art, sport, etc., is also clear in dimensions which are affected by private property.

Third World unemployment as a massive, chronic and universal phenomenon poses fundamental questions to the First World countries. It is one of the indisputable objective facts which brings out the truth of a world which cannot see itself except by stepping outside itself. The 'outsideness' of the Third World shows up and denounces the 'insideness' of the First World. This is something that we do not want to look at because it may drive us mad or convert us from a whole way of being and doing. The ever growing struggle between rich countries (the minority) and poor countries (the majority) not only brings out clearly the inequity of the system and the injustice of international relations but it sets the whole world in a state of tension and conflict which one day will be forced to explode in order to seek a new balance. All this shows that not only the economic order is failing but also the political order and even the whole general project of humanity.

(*c*) The new project of humanity

This general project of humanity can be glimpsed by setting our sights on the kingdom of God from the viewpoint of the reality and the values of the Third World. This does not mean that the kingdom of God, as proclaimed by Jesus, offers a technical model for society nor that the Third World, as it is today, is already a foretaste of what can come to be the kingdom of God among men. On the contrary, there is much that needs changing in the Third World and much thought and work is needed on what the new society should be. Otherwise the kingdom of God would remain a pure Utopia and would cease to be a direction-giving and regulating Utopia, especially in the new project of humanity and civilisation. But on the other hand, a project of humanity and civilisation which did not take the kingdom into account, would be diminished not only in its trancendent projection but also in its historical realisation.

This appeal to the kingdom of God is multiple. But for our purpose it is sufficient to note the following. The kingdom of God, even though it is not reduced to a purely historical project, seeks a historical realisation, requires the world of men to be in conformity with a certain form. Secondly, the will to implant the kingdom of God into human history is an efficacious will on God's part, a will that cannot be a complete fiasco. Finally, although the kingdom of God can be experienced within the individual and must be experienced internally in this way for it to be truly the kingdom of God, it cannot be reduced to the individual level, or even to the level of the community, or the ecclesial level. It extends also to the structural because people's lives depend largely on the social, economic and political structure in which they live.

The kingdom of God points out certain fundamental characteristics for the form of the new society, precisely in relation to this problem of unemployment. Let us mention some of the most important of these characteristics.

The first of these is that the poor have a preferential place in the kingdom of God. The poorest of the poor are the unemployed, especially when they never have access to work or that access is totally insufficient. From the point of view of the Christian God, the poor have the most special place in the Utopia which is the kingdom of God, which means that the human order that corresponds to the kingdom of God must be built round the poor and for the poor. In biblical revelation there are two main reasons for this: that they are the most unfortunate, and that they are the ones who can obtain God's blessing because they have the attitudes which make possible the best relations with God and other men. In historical analysis there is another decisive reason: they are the majority of humanity, at least if we include those who do not have work suited to their capacities and their needs. This means that both for theological reasons and from the most positive point of view we must structure the social reality to take into account the primary fact of the poor and, in our case, the unemployed.

The second characteristic is that the order of values which shapes this world must be changed for another order in accord with its real needs and the perspective of the kingdom. If we examine the present course of history, we find that its characteristics are completely contrary to the characteristics of the kingdom. Blessed are the rich and cursed are the poor; getting and accumulating is preferred in every way to giving and sharing; dominating and being served is regarded as better than serving and giving freedom; anxiety about the transitory and superficial is thought more important than caring about the deep and the permanent. . . . And so we could go on. As against the worship of God as the fundamental horizon which relativises everything else, the time which brings out all that is most human in us, there are the idolatries of our world, the idolatry of wealth, the idolatry of power, the idolatry of consumption, the idolatry of egoism. . . . All this leads among other things to the monopolisation of work as a source of wealth, power, etc., making it more difficult to share its possibilities, even though a rational division of labour would give us all a much greater capacity for self-realisation through more free time which would not all be spent in diversion and rest but in creative, unpaid work which could increase our humanity and also humanity in general. It does not seem irrational to proclaim that the perspectives of the kingdom of God are much more humanising than the perspectives of this present world.

The third characteristic implies working for a civilisation of poverty, in which poverty would not be the deprivation of necessary and fundamental needs, a deprivation caused by the historical action of social groups or classes and nations or alliances of nations. Poverty would be a universal state of things, in which the satisfaction of fundamental needs was guaranteed, and also the freedom of personal choice and an atmosphere of personal and communal creativity, which would allow for the appearance of new forms of life and culture, new relations with nature, other people, ourselves and God. Unemployment would not be debasing, if there was a new structuring of society, in which value was set not only or principally upon work called productive but also upon creative work for society. We do not need to return to the Greek world in which those who worked with their hands did not think and those who thought did not work with their hands, or to the medieval world where contemplation and artistic work were regarded as superior to manual work or to incipient commercial work. We need to seek a new balance in which people are not subjected to economic laws but economic laws are subject to people. It is very possible that in the present civilisation of wealth and consumption there is no other answer to unemployment except the creation of new jobs and consequently the promotion of incessant consumerism, even counting with the positive factor that saving can represent as a basic condition for new investments. But are not the principles of a civilisation of wealth being shaken by the very reality of the facts, just as they were pilloried by the proclamation of the kingdom of God made by Jesus to the poor? Material superfluity is in contradiction with spiritual superfluity and it is in this spiritual superfluity that there is a true rest, creative freedom, free time, the necessary condition for all deep freedom.

In the Third World people do not arrive easily at the truth 'and yet only one thing is necessary' but they certainly do arrive more easily at the conviction that few things are strictly necessary. They also arrive at the conviction that something is going very wrong in the (dominant) world when things are so bad in the much greater part of the world, that which is dominated. Things are bad in the dominated world, especially from the material point of view, the dominant world is going wrong especially from the human point of view. Perhaps the fundamental task of solidarity in which the strength of the dominant world was given to improving the work relations in the dominated world could represent a change in the dark course of history. If not even unemployment can be resolved in a world which sees work as the single or principal ingredient of 'value', something very bad indeed is happening.

All this may seem paradoxical. It may seem that it sounds more in favour of unemployment than work. Not so. It is trying to suggest another form of work which could reduce the debasing forms of unemployment. The First World should not adopt a solution to 'its' unemployment without taking into account the effects that this solution has on the majority of humanity. It should not adopt a solution as if the First World was something closed in upon itself without pressing obligations to the rest, the majority, of humanity. The Utopia of the kingdom of God can serve as a light to show the ultimately axiological causes of unemployment and to open new horizons which lead to the new heaven and new earth, in which the values, attitudes and realities of the kingdom of God will prevail over the values, attitudes and realities of the kingdom of Evil.

Translated by Dinah Livingstone

Contributors

JOSÉ BEOZZO was born in 1941, and ordained in 1964. He studied philosophy in São Paulo and theology at the Gregorianum, then sociology and communications at Louvain. He is a director of the Theological Institute of Lins in Brazil, and also lectures in theology at the university of São Paulo. He has published articles in journals all over Latin America, and has contributed to Vol. II/2 of the History of the Church in Latin America, published in 1980, and to 'Materials for a History of Theology in Latin America' (1981). He is Brazilian co-ordinator of CEHILA, the Commission for Historical Studies on the Church in Latin America.

IGNACIO ELLACURIA was born in the Basque country. He has lived in Latin America since 1949. He studied theology with Rahner at Innsbruck (1958-1962) and obtained a PhD with a thesis on the thought of Zubiri. He is currently director of the El Salvador Centre for Theological Reflection. His most recent publication is *Freedom made Flesh* (1976). He is a regular contributor to El Salvador and foreign periodicals.

WALTER FERNANDES is director of research at the Indian Social Institute, New Delhi. His most recent books include *Participatory Research and Evaluation* (1981); *Caste and Conversion Movements* (1981); *The Indian Catholic Community* (1980).

IRING FETSCHER was born in 1922 in Marbach, Neckar, and studied at the universities of Tübingen and Paris. His thesis for the doctorate was about Hegel's anthropology whilst that for his licence to teach in the university on Rousseau's political philosophy. Since 1963 he has been professor of political science and social philosophy at the university of Frankfurt-am-Main. His principal books are *Von Marx zur Sowjetideologie* (1956, [23]1981); *Karl Marx et le Marxisme* (1967); *Rousseaus politische Philosophie* (1960); *Modelle der Friedenssicherung* (1972); *Ueberlebensbedingungen der Menscheit* (1980). He has been visiting professor at Göttingen, Nijmegen, Tel Aviv, and the Graduate Faculty of the New School for Social Research, New York.

ANDRÉ GORZ was born in Vienna in 1924 and since 1960 he has been one of the editors of *Temps Modernes*, the journal founded by Jean-Paul Sartre. He writes as a journalist under the pseudonym of Michel Bosquet. His principal works include: *Strategy for Labor* (Boston 1967); *Socialism and Revolution* (New York 1973); *Critique du Capitalisme quotidien* (Paris 1973), written under the name of Michel Bosquet; *The Division of Labour* (Brighton 1976); *Fondements pour une morale* (Paris 1977); *Ecology as Politics* (Boston 1980); *Farewell to the Proletariat* (London 1982).

EUGENE HEIMLER was trained as Psychiatric Social Worker in England. He worked for Middlesex County Council for seventeen years and pioneered the Hendon Experiment and the Hounslow Project. He worked all throughout his professional life in the area of unemployed. He taught human relations and social functioning at London University for twenty years. He was appointed as consultant (after he evolved his Scale of Social Functioning) to the World Health Organistion and to the Government of the United States. He was also advisor to the Ministry of Social Security in Great Britain on issues concerning unemployment. He has been professor of human social functioning at the university of Calgary, Alberta, Canada, for the past fourteen years and he is teaching his approach in many countries. His publications include: *A Link in the Chain* (London 1962); *Mental Illness and Social Work* (Ringwood, Victoria, Australia: Penguin Pelican Books, 1967); *Resistance Against Tyranny–a Symposium* (London 1967); *Survival in Society* (London 1975); *Concentration Camp* (London 1979).

FRIEDHELM HENGSBACH, SJ, was born in Dortmund in 1937 and joined the Society of Jesus in 1957. He studied theology and economics at Munich, Frankfurt and Bochum. He lectures in economic and social ethics at St George's Institute of Philosophy and Theology, Frankfurt-am-Main. His works include: *Die Assoziierung afrikanischer Staaten an die Europäischen Gemeinschaften. Eine Politik raumwirtschaftlicher Integration* (1977); (editor of) *Aussperrung und Streik. Ungleiche Mittel* (1980); *Die Arbeit hat Vorrang. Eine Option katholischer Soziallehre* (1982). His articles include 'Drei Typen katholischer Soziallehre' in *Orientierung* 46 (1982).

RONALD KRIETEMEYER is currently director of the Office of Domestic Social Development at the United States Catholic Conference. This is the staff office responsible for advising and assisting the Catholic bishops at the national level on domestic social policy issues. He previously served for two years as the staff specialist on urban issues for that same office. Between 1973-1978 he worked as the coordinator for Social Justice Affairs in the Catholic Charities office of the Archdiocese of St. Paul and Minneapolis. He had gained a master's degree in public affairs at the Humphrey Institute, University of Minnesota, and a master's degree in theology at St. John's University Collegeville, Minnesota. He is married and lives in the District of Columbia.

GIANNINO PIANA teaches moral theology at the Novara Seminario Vescovile and Christian ethics at the Free University of Urbino. He is the national secretary of ATISM (Associazione teologica italiana per lo studio della morale). His publications include *Principi di morale religiosa* (1972) and *Christiani per il terzo millennio* (1979). He has edited the section on 'moral theology' in the *Dizionario Teologico Interdisciplinare* (1977) and is editor (with G. Ruggieri) of the series *Cronache teologiche* published by Editor Marietti. He is also on the editorial boards of: *Revista di teologia morale, Hermeneutica, Servitium.*

HUGUES PUEL, OP, was born in Bordeaux, France, in 1932 and joined the Dominicans in 1956. Since 1964 he has been active in the association *Economie et Humanisme* as director of its study centre, editor of its review, head of research into the socio-economics of employment and editor of the *North-South* collection. In 1968, after studies at Berkeley, California, he gained a doctorate with a thesis on the controversies among American economists on the nature and causes of unemployment. Since 1970 he has taught political economy, labour economics and development economics at the university of Lyons, France. His publications include *Chômage et capitalisme contemporains* (1971); *Les Économistes radicaux aux USA* (1974); *En finir avec le chômage* (1979); *Physionomies de la ville* (1982).

ALFRED DE SOUZA is director, Indian Social Institute and editor of *Social Action*. His books include *The Urban Poor* (1980); *Women in Contemporary India and South Asia* (1981); *The Social Organisation of Aging Among the Urban Poor* (1982).

CONCILIUM

1. (Vol. 1 No. 1) **Dogma.** Ed. Edward Schillebeeckx. 86pp.
2. (Vol. 2 No. 1) **Liturgy.** Ed. Johannes Wagner. 100pp.
3. (Vol. 3 No. 1) **Pastoral.** Ed. Karl Rahner. 104pp.
4. (Vol. 4 No. 1) **Ecumenism.** Hans Küng. 108pp.
5. (Vol. 5 No. 1) **Moral Theology.** Ed. Franz Bockle 98pp.
6. (Vol. 6 No. 1) **Church and World.** Ed. Johannes Baptist Metz. 92pp.
7. (Vol. 7 No. 1) **Church History.** Roger Aubert. 92pp.
8. (Vol. 8 No. 1) **Canon Law.** Ed. Teodoro Jimenez Urresti and Neophytos Edelby. 96pp.
9. (Vol. 9 No. 1) **Spirituality.** Ed. Christian Duquoc. 88pp.
10. (Vol. 10 No. 1) **Scripture.** Ed. Pierre Benoit and Roland Murphy. 92pp.
11. (Vol. 1 No. 2) **Dogma.** Ed. Edward Schillebeeckx. 88pp.
12. (Vol. 2 No. 2) **Liturgy.** Ed. Johannes Wagner. 88pp.
13. (Vol. 3 No. 2) **Pastoral.** Ed. Karl Rahner. 84pp.
14. (Vol. 4 No. 2) **Ecumenism.** Ed. Hans Küng. 96pp.
15. (Vol. 5 No. 2) **Moral Theology.** Ed. Franz Bockle. 88pp.
16. (Vol. 6 No. 2) **Church and World.** Ed. Johannes Baptist Metz. 84.pp.
17. (Vol. 7 No. 2) **Church History.** Ed. Roger Aubert. 96pp.
18. (Vol. 8 No. 2) **Religious Freedom.** Ed. Neophytos Edelby and Teodoro Jimenez Urresti. 96pp.
19. (Vol. 9 No. 2) **Religionless Christianity?** Ed. Christian Duquoc. 96pp.
20. (Vol. 10 No. 2) **The Bible and Tradition.** Ed. Pierre Benoit and Roland E. Murphy. 96pp.
21. (Vol. 1 No 3) **Revelation and Dogma.** Ed. Edward Schillebeeckx. 88pp.
22. (Vol. 2 No. 3) **Adult Baptism and Initiation.** Ed. Johannes Wagner. 96pp.
23. (Vol. 3 No. 3) **Atheism and Indifference.** Ed. Karl Rahner. 92pp.
24. (Vol. 4 No. 3) **The Debate on the Sacraments.** Ed. Hans Küng. 92pp.
25. (Vol. 5 No. 3) **Morality, Progress and History.** Ed. Franz Bockle. 84pp.
26. (Vol. 6 No. 3) **Evolution.** Ed. Johannes Baptist Metz. 88pp.
27. (Vol. 7 No. 3) **Church History.** Ed. Roger Aubert. 92pp.
28. (Vol. 8 No. 3) **Canon Law—Theology and Renewal.** Ed. Neophytos Edelby and Teodoro Jimenez Urresti. 92pp.
29. (Vol. 9 No. 3) **Spirituality and Politics.** Ed. Christian Duquoc. 84pp.
30. (Vol. 10 No. 3) **The Value of the Old Testament.** Ed. Pierre Benoit and Roland Murphy. 92pp.
31. (Vol. 1 No. 4) **Man, World and Sacrament.** Ed. Edward Schillebeeckx. 84pp.
32. (Vol. 2 No. 4) **Death and Burial: Theology and Liturgy.** Ed. Johannes Wagner. 88pp.
33. (Vol. 3 No. 4) **Preaching the Word of God.** Ed. Karl Rahner. 96pp.
34. (Vol. 4 No. 4) **Apostolic by Succession?** Ed. Hans Küng. 96pp.
35. (Vol. 5 No. 4) **The Church and Social Morality.** Ed. Franz Bockle. 92pp.
36. (Vol. 6 No. 4) **Faith and the World of Politics.** Ed. Johannes Baptist Metz 96pp.
37. (Vol. 7 No. 4) **Prophecy.** Ed. Roger Aubert. 80pp.
38. (Vol. 8 No. 4) **Order and the Sacraments.** Ed. Neophytos Edelby and Teodoro Jimenez Urresti. 96pp.
39. (Vol. 9 No. 4) **Christian Life and Eschatology.** Ed. Christian Duquoc. 94pp.
40. (Vol. 10 No. 4) **The Eucharist: Celebrating the Presence of the Lord.** Ed. Pierre Benoit and Roland Murphy. 88pp.
41. (Vol. 1 No. 5) **Dogma.** Ed. Edward Schillebeeckx. 84pp.
42. (Vol. 2 No. 5) **The Future of the Liturgy.** Ed. Johannes Wagner. 92pp.
43. (Vol. 3 No. 5) **The Ministry and Life of Priests Today.** Ed. Karl Rahner. 104pp.
44. (Vol. 4 No. 5) **Courage Needed.** Ed. Hans Küng. 92pp.
45. (Vol. 5 No. 5) **Profession and Responsibility in Society.** Ed. Franz Bockle. 84pp.
46. (Vol. 6 No. 5) **Fundamental Theology.** Ed. Johannes Baptist Metz. 84pp.
47. (Vol. 7 No. 5) **Sacralization in the History of the Church.** Ed. Roger Aubert. 80pp.
48. (Vol. 8 No. 5) **The Dynamism of Canon Law.** Ed. Neophytos Edelby and Teodoro Jimenez Urresti. 92pp.
49. (Vol. 9 No. 5) **An Anxious Society Looks to the Gospel.** Ed. Christian Duquoc. 80pp.
50. (Vol. 10 No. 5) **The Presence and Absence of God.** Ed. Pierre Benoit and Roland Murphy. 88pp.
51. (Vol. 1 No. 6) **Tension between Church and Faith.** Ed. Edward Schillebeeckx. 160pp.
52. (Vol. 2 No. 6) **Prayer and Community.** Ed. Herman Schmidt. 156pp.
53. (Vol. 3 No. 6) **Catechetics for the Future.** Ed. Alois Müller. 168pp.
54. (Vol. 4 No. 6) **Post-Ecumenical Christianity.** Ed. Hans Küng. 168pp.
55. (Vol. 5 No. 6) **The Future of Marriage as Institution.** Ed. Franz Bockle. 180pp.
56. (Vol. 6 No. 6) **Moral Evil Under Challenge.** Ed. Johannes Baptist Metz. 160pp.
57. (Vol. 7 No. 6) **Church History at a Turning Point.** Ed. Roger Aubert. 160pp.
58. (Vol. 8 No. 6) **Structures of the Church's Presence in the World of Today.** Ed. Teodoro Jimenez Urresti. 160pp.
59. (Vol. 9 No. 6) **Hope.** Ed. Christian Duquoc. 160pp.
60. (Vol. 10 No. 6) **Immortality and Resurrection.** Ed. Pierre Benoit and Roland Murphy. 160pp.
61. (Vol. 1 No. 7) **The S… Administration of Re…** Ed. Edward Schillebe… 160pp.
62. (Vol. 2 No. 7) **Worsh… Christian Man Today…** Herman Schmidt. 15…
63. (Vol. 3 No. 7) **Demo… of the Church.** Ed. A… Müller. 160pp.
64. (Vol. 4 No. 7) **The P… Ministry in the Churc…** Hans Küng. 160pp.
65. (Vol. 5 No. 7) **The M… of Man.** Ed. Franz B… 144pp.
66. (Vol. 6 No. 7) **Funda… Theology in the Chur…** Johannes Baptist Met…
67. (Vol. 7 No. 7) **The Self-Understanding of … Church.** Ed. Roger A… 144pp.
68. (Vol. 8 No. 7) **Conte… the Church.** Ed. Teo… Jimenez Urresti. 152p…
69. (Vol. 9 No. 7) **Spiritu… Public or Private?** Ed… Duquoc. 156pp.
70. (Vol. 10 No. 7) **Theol… Exegesis and Proclam…** Roland Murphy. 144p…
71. (Vol. 1 No. 8) **The B… the Unity of the Chur…** Edward Schillebeeckx…
72. (Vol. 2 No. 8) **Liturg… Ministry.** Ed. Herma… 160pp.
73. (Vol. 3 No. 8) **Reform… Church.** Ed. Alois M… Norbert Greinacher.
74. (Vol. 4 No. 8) **Mutua… Recognition of Ecclesi… Ministries?** Ed. Hans … Walter Kasper. 152p…
75. (Vol. 5 No. 8) **Man i… Society.** Ed. Franz Bo… 160pp.
76. (Vol. 6 No. 8) **The G… Question.** Ed. Johann… Metz. 156pp.
77. (Vol. 7 No. 8) **Electio… Consensus-Reception.** … Giuseppe Alberigo a… Weiler. 156pp.
78. (Vol. 8 No. 8) **Celiba… Catholic Priest.** Ed. W… Bassett and Peter Hu… 160pp.
79. (Vol. 9 No. 8) **Prayer…** Christian Duquoc and… Geffré. 126pp.
80. (Vol. 10 No. 8) **Minis… Church.** Ed. Bas van … Roland Murphy. 152p…
81. **The Persistence of Re…** Andrew Greeley and … Baum. 0 8164 2537 X …
82. **Liturgical Experience …** Ed. Herman Schmidt … Power. 0 8164 2538 8 …
83. **Truth and Certainty.** … Edward Schillebeeckx … van Iersel. 0 8164 253…
84. **Political Commitment … Christian Community.** … Müller and Norbert G… 0 8164 2540 X 156pp.
85. **The Crisis of Religiou…** Ed. Johannes Baptist … Jean-Pierre Jossua. 0 8164 2541 8 144pp.
86. **Humanism and Christ…**

e Geffré. 0 8164 2542 6
.
uture of Christian
age. Ed. William Bassett
eter Huizing.
4 2575 2.
zation in the Church. Ed.
Küng and Walter Kasper.
4 2572 8 156pp.
ual Revivals. Ed. Christian
oc and Casiano Floristán.
4 2573 6 156pp.
and the Word of God.
ranz Bockle and Jacques
Pohier.
4 2574 4 156pp.
hurch as Institution. Ed.
ry Baum and Andrew
ey. 0 8164 2575 2 168pp.
s and Liturgy. Ed.
an Schmidt and David
r. 0 8164 2576 0 156pp.
Christ and Human
om. Ed. Edward
ebeeckx and Bas van
. 0 8164 2577 9 168pp.
xperience of Dying. Ed.
ert Greinacher and Alois
r. 0 8164 2578 7 156pp.
ogy of Joy. Ed. Johannes
st Metz and Jean-Pierre
a. 0 8164 2579 5 164pp.
Aystical and Political
nsion of the Christian
Ed. Claude Geffré and
vo Guttierez.
4 2580 9 168pp.
uture of the Religious Life.
eter Huizing and William
tt. 0 8164 2094 7 96pp.
tians and Jews. Ed. Hans
and Walter Kasper.
4 2095 5 96pp.
rience of the Spirit. Ed.
Huizing and William
tt. 0 8164 2096 3 144pp.
lity in Contemporary
licism. Ed. Franz Bockle
acques Marie Pohier.
4 2097 1 126pp.
city. Ed. Andrew Greeley
Gregory Baum.
4 2145 5 120pp.
gy and Cultural Religious
tions. Ed. Herman Schmidt
David Power. 0 8164 2146 2
.
rsonal God? Ed. Edward
ebeeckx and Bas van
. 0 8164 2149 8 142pp.
Poor and the Church. Ed.
ert Greinacher and Alois
r. 0 8164 2147 1 128pp.
tianity and Socialism. Ed.
nnes Baptist Metz and
Pierre Jossua.
4 2148 X 144pp.
Churches of Africa: Future
ects. Ed. Claude Geffré
Bertrand Luneau.
4 2150 1 128pp.
ment in the Church. Ed.
am Bassett and Peter
ng. 0 8164 2166 8 128pp.
Did God Make Me? Ed.
Küng and Jürgen
mann. 0 8164 2167 6 112pp.

109. **Charisms in the Church.** Ed. Christian Duquoc and Casiano Floristán. 0 8164 2168 4 128pp.
110. **Moral Formation and Christianity.** Ed. Franz Bockle and Jacques Marie Pohier. 0 8164 2169 2 120pp.
111. **Communication in the Church.** Ed. Gregory Baum and Andrew Greeley. 0 8164 2170 6 126pp.
112. **Liturgy and Human Passage.** Ed. David Power and Luis Maldonado. 0 8164 2608 2 136pp.
113. **Revelation and Experience.** Ed. Edward Schillebeeckx and Bas van Iersel. 0 8164 2609 0 134pp.
114. **Evangelization in the World Today.** Ed. Norbert Greinacher and Alois Müller. 0 8164 2610 4 136pp.
115. **Doing Theology in New Places.** Ed. Jean-Pierre Jossua and Johannes Baptist Metz. 0 8164 2611 2 120pp.
116. **Buddhism and Christianity.** Ed. Claude Geffré and Mariasusai Dhavamony. 0 8164 2612 0 136pp.
117. **The Finances of the Church.** Ed. William Bassett and Peter Huizing. 0 8164 2197 8 160pp.
118. **An Ecumenical Confession of Faith?** Ed. Hans Küng and Jürgen Moltmann. 0 8164 2198 6 136pp.
119. **Discernment of the Spirit and of Spirits.** Ed. Casiano Floristán and Christian Duquoc. 0 8164 2199 4 136pp.
120. **The Death Penalty and Torture.** Ed. Franz Bockle and Jacques Marie Pohier. 0 8164 2200 1 136pp.
121. **The Family in Crisis or in Transition.** Ed. Andrew Greely. 0 567 30001 3 128pp.
122. **Structures of Initiation in Crisis.** Ed. Luis Maldonado and David Power. 0 567 30002 1 128pp.
123. **Heaven.** Ed. Bas van Iersel and Edward Schillebeeckx. 0 567 30003 X 120pp.
124. **The Church and the Rights of Man.** Ed. Alois Müller and Norbert Greinacher. 0 567 30004 8 140pp.
125. **Christianity and the Bourgeoisie.** Ed. Johannes Baptist Metz. 0 567 30005 6 144pp.
126. **China as a Challenge to the Church.** Ed. Claude Geffré and Joseph Spae. 0 567 30006 4 136pp.
127. **The Roman Curia and the Communion of Churches.** Ed. Peter Huizing and Knut Walf. 0 567 30007 2 144pp.
128. **Conflicts about the Holy Spirit.** Ed. Hans Küng and Jürgen Moltmann. 0 567 30008 0 144pp.
129. **Models of Holiness.** Ed. Christian Duquoc and Casiano Floristán. 0 567 30009 9 128pp.
130. **The Dignity of the Despised of the Earth.** Ed. Jacques Marie Pohier and Dietmar Mieth. 0 567 30010 2 144pp.
131. **Work and Religion.** Ed. Gregory Baum. 0 567 30011 0 148pp.
132. **Symbol and Art in Worship.** Ed. Luis Maldonado and David Power. 0 567 30012 9 136pp.
133. **Right of the Community to a Priest.** Ed. Edward Schillebeeckx and Johannes Baptist Metz. 0 567 30013 7 148pp.
134. **Women in a Men's Church.** Ed. Virgil Elizondo and Norbert Greinacher. 0 567 30014 5 144pp.
135. **True and False Universality of Christianity.** Ed. Claude Geffré and Jean-Pierre Jossua. 0 567 30015 3 138pp.
136. **What is Religion? An Inquiry for Christian Theology.** Ed. Mircea Eliade and David Tracy. 0 567 30016 1 98pp.
137. **Electing our Own Bishops.** Ed. Peter Huizing and Knut Walf. 0 567 30017 X 112pp.
138. **Conflicting Ways of Interpreting the Bible.** Ed. Hans Küng and Jürgen Moltmann. 0 567 30018 8 112pp.
139. **Christian Obedience.** Ed. Casiano Floristán and Christian Duquoc. 0 567 30019 6 96pp.
140. **Christian Ethics and Economics: the North-South Conflict.** Ed. Dietmar Mieth and Jacques Marie Pohier. 0 567 30020 X 128pp.

1981

141. **Neo-Conservatism: Social and Religious Phenomenon.** Ed. Gregory Baum and John Coleman. 0 567 30021 8.
142. **The Times of Celebration.** Ed. David Power and Mary Collins. 0 567 30022 6.
143. **God as Father.** Ed. Edward Schillebeeckx and Johannes Baptist Metz. 0 567 30023 4.
144. **Tensions Between the Churches of the First World and the Third World.** Ed. Virgil Elizondo and Norbert Greinacher. 0 567 30024 2.
145. **Nietzsche and Christianity.** Ed. Claude Geffré and Jean-Pierre Jossua. 0 567 30025 0.
146. **Where Does the Church Stand?** Ed. Giuseppe Alberigo. 0 567 30026 9.
147. **The Revised Code of Canon Law: a Missed Opportunity?** Ed. Peter Huizing and Knut Walf. 0 567 30027 7.
148. **Who Has the Say in the Church?** Ed. Hans Küng and Jürgen Moltmann. 0 567 30028 5.
149. **Francis of Assisi Today.** Ed. Casiano Floristán and Christian Duquoc. 0 567 30029 3.
150. **Christian Ethics: Uniformity, Universality, Pluralism.** Ed. Jacques Pohier and Dietmar Mieth. 0 567 30030 7.

ack issues are still in print and available for sale. Orders should be sent to the publishers,

T. & T. CLARK LIMITED

36 George Street, Edinburgh EH2 2LQ, Scotland